THE ALTERNATIVE SOCIETY

THE ALTERNATIVE SOCIETY

Software for the Nineteen-Eighties

de Cronin Hastings

Timeliness is best in all matters.

Hesiod

David & Charles

Newton Abbot   London   North Pomfret (Vt)

To

HRH

British Library Cataloguing in Publication Data

Hastings, De Cronin
 The alternative society.
 1. Economic policy
 I. Title
 330.9   HD82

 ISBN 0-7153-7880-5

Typeset by Northampton Phototypesetters Limited
and printed in Great Britain
by Redwood Burn Limited, Trowbridge and Esher
for David & Charles (Publishers) Limited
Brunel House Newton Abbot Devon

Published in the United States of America
by David & Charles Inc
North Pomfret Vermont 05053 USA

CONTENTS

INTRODUCTION

Ah, Love! Could thou and I with fate conspire
To grasp this sorry Scheme of Things entire
Would not we shatter it to bits – and then
Remould it nearer to the heart's desire.

Edward Fitzgerald

In the world of high-tech the word *hardware* covers the actual items of agrochemistry and microtechnology. *Software* takes care of the programming that monitors the behaviour of these jewels. Contrary to received opinion computers are amazingly consistent animals. Most of their errors (which are many) spring from faulty programming or as the programmers themselves say $GI = GO$ – garbage *in* equals garbage *out* – an equation which, transferred to the political arena, accounts for many of the other vicissitudes of man. He – man – apart from drinking when he isn't thirsty (Beaumarchais) is rather a responsible number, yet the software of our age still remains alarmingly and irresponsibly primitive as the present argument tries to show. In case that argument seems also alarmingly and irresponsibly obscure the following summary offers a digest of the book's order of thought which starts at one end of the political spectrum, continues at the other, then fills in the alternatives between; on the presumption that somewhere along the line our shortcomings as software buffs will make themselves felt. An important presumption, in view of the manifest unreadiness of current society to cope with the danger signals of the 'eighties as they pile up like thunder clouds on the Western horizon.

(1) The first pursuit of the millennium was promoted in chapter vii of the Book of Daniel about 165 BC at the height of the Maccabaean revolt.

7

(2) The last can be identified with the puritan revolution and the English Civil War when drunk with prophecy and carried away by Cromwell's burning words the House of Commons declared that 'as before the birth of Christ God's people were aware of the coming of a new world, so let England now be the instrument to complete the divine work by breaking the yoke and removing the burden of sin'. Surprising words to come out of the portly bosoms of 129 (or thereabout) MPs but they believed it was the destiny of the English to bring in a New Order which would revolutionize the political, social and economic history of mankind. They even enlarged the Fleet (ten times) to prepare as they said for the Coming of Christ.

(3) To most of us now this all seems funny ha-ha but our built-in pessimism is a very recent growth, founded largely on the failure of science to change human nature which in Francis Bacon's Utopia as opposed to Thomas Moore's it was confidently expected to do. Oddly. Every other animal on earth is happy to be neither more nor less than what he is. Only man – man only – rebels against his destiny. Chased out of Eden he perpetually snuffles after Parousia, the Promised Land. Or did until materialist geography demonstrated that there was no such country; and its literature that the proper end of human effort is (in the free world) the development of constitutional democracy. Human rights.

(4) In this light consider the Civil War, treated almost without exception by historians *not* as a volcanic eruption, an ingressio, advent of a new thing, but as a hiccup, unseemly enough, alas, in the stately progress of the British Constitution towards its own Balmoral. *Interregnum* is the word widely used of the Protectorate, meaning the event-ful non-event that wasted 30 or so years of parliamentary time between the death of homosexual Jamie and the return of heterosexual Charlie.

(5) Fair enough if you regard the history of England as essentially a struggle between heter and homo – Parliament and Crown. But if per contra you see our current disarray as a consequence of the national preoccupation with precisely that kind of side-kick, and the inability of the West to find a slogan that will unite the Third World against communism as a consequence of its own loss of direction, the vital need seems to be to make some effort to think again.

6) To think again amongst other things about another side-kick dear to the West, its reaction to Marx and Marxism, a creed which now counts more heads and hearts than Christianity. For his own purposes Marx transferred his feud with the bourgeoisie to the field of economics, at the time a masterstroke or so it seemed. But in the event through what one can only suppose to have been a deliberate mistake, he made it possible for others to construct a simple but massive and (as we suggest) unanswerable refutation of his whole economic philosophy. One only has to accept Malthus on 'the greatest principle of economics' to perceive that the Marxist interpretation is even in its own first premise nowhere on target; on the contrary an act of the lowest gamesmanship by a grand master of the highest.

(7) This book is not an attack on Marxism; the grand master is included in our critique merely to illustrate the depths of confusion to which the free world has sunk. While the British have lost a world empire the USSR has built a new one *in Europe* and is coming on nicely in Asia and Africa not to mention S. America and the Middle East. What we need is what our adversary has – a story – a story that will bring conviction to those who would like to remain our friends but are not sure whether that is going to pay.

(8) This story such as it is can be put as well in economic terms as any other. Better perhaps, because economics provides the medium in which the Third World can start talks with the First or anyway get within range, even when the issues are, like child-birth, not primarily economic. The greatest threat to our future lies in the world population explosion under which though the human race has to date squeezed its 4,000 million into less than 12% of the globe's surface, world population is doubling every 35 years (8,000 million by AD 2010).

(9) This threat only an economics of scarcity can cure – by a catastrophe for which this book has no remedy. For many others, however, the argument suggests that a simple readjustment of the economic system will remove their capacity to make trouble. Strikes, trade union confrontation with government, cost-plus inflation, shop floor alienation, automation, cybernetics, pollution, giantism, the bureaucracy,

overconcentration of population, low labour costs in the Third World, proliferation of nuclear weaponry, stress symptoms, hooliganism, vandalism, the shadow of the totalitarians, *anomie* – these and many more can be robbed of their sting. As for unemployment it can be sunk without trace.

(10) And, as the locust plague of microchips will soon make plain, to believe that automation like mass production will eventually make more rather than less employment, is unrealistic. *Automation* is a word meaning let's make it without human hands. *Full employment* is two words meaning we all want to put our human hands to work because our wage packets depend upon our working as human hands. Hence the quandary of the century. The truth is, full automation and full employment, though immaculate objectives, are mutually exclusive, as even our politicians must realize by now. One or the other must go; and since neither is prepared to exit gracefully it means that the existing economic system will have to be made to bend, if only slightly. More accurately, straighten. This book bends or straightens the system with results that will evoke (as it maintains) the total submergence of unemployment in what can properly be called *the alternative society*.

Saint

THE PROVIDENT SOCIETY

To everthing there is a season and a time
to every purpose under the heaven.

Ecclesiastes iii : i

I

MICAWBER'S LAW

Those Nasturtiums

₋ong before Monty Python's Flying Circus held a debate on the ₋ssue a letter arrived for Proust one morning from an American ₋irl who, after living with *Recherche* for three years and failing to ₋et the message, now urged him to come to the point. 'Tell me', ₋he ordered, 'in two lines what you wish to say.'

Proust remained unresponsive, *Recherche* being in both his and Monty Python's view the wrong medium for a two-line digest. Some themes, however, respond to such treatment and since the ₋ith of its message can be transmitted in less than two lines – two ₋words – *essential concordance* – coined by ETA Hoffmann (of the 'Tales') – this book should be one of them.

There may of course be American girls who consider two words ₋excessive; in which case (provided this is the last and final demand – no further order can be accepted) we offer with infinite cordiality one word. This time by way of Swedenborg who can be said to have earned its perpetual copyright – *correspondences*. A doctrine, passionately held by many people, from Plotinus to that most folksy of savants, the Seer of Poughkeepsie. Baudelaire, however, divining as he did in a moment of inspiration the significance of Hoffmann's surprising confession that the odour of red or brown nasturtiums always made him hear 'afar off' the 'grave deep note of an oboe', is for our present purpose its most influential exponent. For here at one blow in the phrase already quoted, his own, lay the precedent for the kind of vocabulary the arts had always needed and never had: an *essential concordance*: between colours, tastes, sounds, smells and the tactile experience, variations upon which most of the others are. On that foundation, and fortified with Swedenborg's Correspondences, Fourier's Analogies and large quantities of hasheesh, Baudelaire set out to make the Latin quarters of Europe concordance-minded. All phenomena are allegories, went the argument, transparent symbols of a greater *or* revealed in the *correspondences* between things. Various critics Hogarth and Burke amongst them, had toyed with the nee (shipshape), but it was left to the great aesthetes of the nineteent century to regularize the analogy habit, the habit of analysing on art in the terms of another, thereby enriching the vocabularie of all.

It worked. It worked like magic. Music acquired texture, colour sang, plots smelt, lavatory jokes were blue, Devon Pixies left a bac taste in the mouth. As for the vine it acquired from the clas battle its own specialized vocabulary after the style of Thurber' naive domestic Burgundy without any breeding whose patron would be amused by its presumption.

Thus was modern art criticism born and with it a principle tha according to the present argument has a right to fly higher than th wine-cellar or the ateliers frequented by Baudelaire and hi equivocal friends – so long as those who use it do not abuse it in for instance, the concept of the *process of history*, streamlined by Marx and fellow-travellers into a sort of Royal Train moving through the ages on rails that will end up in History's good time at Karlmoral, Stalinshire. Not quite the same kind of *essentia concordance*, this, applying as it does to something rather different, a theory of history that springs from a dialectically based evolution involving the ingurgitation of one event by its opposite, so that all can be seen as related in time, a tie-up that gives high satisfaction to reason.

And to nothing else. Certainly not to experience. Let us here and now claim in the strongest possible words that this picture is blarney and blarney of a high order. As every specialist knows the historic process is arm-chair made, the work of a sedentary salvage corps of back-room boys who see their job as a rescue operation mounted to pluck continuity from a past composed of innumerable non-sequitors, bouleversements, tangental departures. Revolutions so-called. Miscalled. A revolution is precisely what every revolution is *not*. For the simplest of reasons; events concede one constant or essential concordance only: their incalculability. No question of a dialectic; on the contrary, except in the eye of God and Providence both of whom remain inscrutable, a crazy quilt of alien elements united in one object only, to reject any principle of continuity other than those coined in post-prandial pranks by the sedentary salvage corps.

Hence all we can really expect of the future as opposed to a past rearranged and thus trumped up by the pranksters, is that something unexpected will turn up. Micawber's Law let's call it, founded on the probabilities of the case rather than on the genius of human nature for out-smarting itself. Or as Cromwell would have put it, Providence. A totally unreliable dame. When one evening in the late 1780s a young French aristocrat stood on the quays of Rouen watching the unloading of two outsize iron hoops from England he had every reason to believe in the stability of his own revolution, known to us as the Enlightenment. With hindsight he would have realized that the Age of Reason could not, at that moment, have been in greater jeopardy had those hoops been filled with strontium 90. Product of no less than three, maybe four revolutions ahead. Earthshakers all. Each alien to the others in degree or kind. Each putting paid to its predecessor. Each destined to mature during his own lifetime and throw it into confusion. None as yet revealed to him or his society.

Standing midway between the Encyclopedists and the blue-devils, he probably saw the future of civilization through the eye of *exaltés* like Madame de Staël as the measured tread of a whole society towards rationalism – enlightenment – in which man would at last free man from ignorance, tyranny, superstition, bondage of one sort or another. Within a matter of months he was a refugee fleeing from the Terror; within years, when the first Napoleon and the third revolution had exhausted themselves, he was to become one of the engineers of the fourth, since called the Industrial: Sir Mark Brunel, Thames tunneller, sire to the Great Western Railway and Great Eastern Steamship.

A turn-up more startling than the transition from eighteenth-century Reason to the mad elephants of Coketown, from *Phèdre* at Coppet to the bellying steam of the GWR, would be hard to find outside the petards waiting in our own day to hoist the engineers of Canaveral and California. Micawber, an optimist and a Victorian, expected the unexpected to turn up a golden guinea or two, but the world's anticipations today are more lean; less golden; qualifying perhaps for Alvin Toffler's *Future Shock* or Professor K. Boulding's system breaks. Shock philosophies both, which, well though they fit our present insecurities, do raise the inexorable question: from what break? To what system? Unless of course – which despite everything said above isn't really to be ruled out – we happen to come into possession of a system that doesn't break; or, rather, a principle that holds good throughout the thunder of breaking systems.

Do we at whatever level, degraded or otherwise, know of any principle that could be said to tolerate non-sequitors and system breaks insofar as to find them an acceptable risk; survive them; involve them even. Discover an essential concordance even?

Dissatisfied Animal

Not a *principle* perhaps, conceivably a *principal*. The very party we have been discussing, the one constant – why not – in all these breakages – homo sapiens sapiens* none other. The only animal on earth who keeps making systems, then, in a persistent effort to upstage God, the Devil, nature, process, providence, fate, fratricide, history, breaking them.

Marx saw sapiens as the slave of evolution when he is in fact its enfant terrible. Here we come to the nub or crux of the human predicament, a nub or crux that disposes once for all of *historic process*, at least as a Royal Train Balmoral bound. For the surprising thing is and it really is rather extraordinary, all these systems – or system breaks – all these discontinuities, all these tangents and bouleversements, all these incalculables do spring as we have already said from the only constant in the situation – man. Do reveal in his perennially eccentric behaviour a genuine concordance, a universal principle, an underlyign unity, a common purpose, definable as – not to overstate the case – wishful thinking. Unlike other animals, who never question their lot, man lives and nourishes that pipe-dream of the good life (or the goods life – economics' variant on the theme) once attained, now lost, but re-attainable for any member of the species capable of the urge. To other animals urges are not unknown, who from time to time chew each other up, yet this rage of sapiens shows nothing they can relate to, well satisfied as they are to be neither more nor less than *what* they are.

Man, per contra, is always lusting to be otherwise. Black-balled from one club, Eden, he queues up for admission to any others that happen to be going, Zion, Promised Land, New Jerusalem, Utopia, Arcadia, Parousia, Cockaigne, New Deal, the Millennium, the Hesperides, Der Tag, the Golden Age. The good time just around the next corner.

Or just around the last. Oddly, we still look back as well as forward – to the good old days – only to be equally unsighted. By a corner. That corner is scarcity corner of which more later. Sufficient for the moment to establish the surprising fact that through all inconsistencies and corners those clubs remain man's

*Anthropologists use the double *sapiens* to distinguish modern man.

perpetual heliport. Put in plain terms we are all misfits in a world that only offers a choice between two unendurable alternatives, 'life' and 'death', either one of which makes the other insufferable. Far from submitting to this fate or as other animals do taking it for granted, we react savagely, searching by way of science, religion, philosophy, drink, drugs, sex, for the break-out or break-in. The break-in to some experience that might reconcile us to death; the break-out by way of challenge to the prison of life.

This, one can be pretty certain, has been the familiar behaviour pattern throughout the six million years in which records of a sort exist of man. Until our own day, that is, when tensions and pressures have got to the point where wishful thinking becomes itself too much like hard work in view of the barrage of problems that threaten to blow the world up. Only alternative now, it seems, is the escape into *anomie*, the torpor that disorients its victims by way of *accidie* and *alienation* and so by insecurity exhausts his will to be.

Not altogether unlovely as an opiate for the people, *anomie*. But there are moments when it is a bad bet and this seems to be one of them. Only because if anything is more certain than another it is that the last quarter of the twentieth century has arrived at some kind of climacteric or system break which demands action. Some, observing the state of society, advocate surgery. But the surgery need not be extensive; indeed, the operation, though drastic, is a relatively simple one.

One precisely, according to the argument of this book. It was always there of course but until our own day no one had the means to implement it. The special significance of the eighties – the opportunity that now gives the word *climacteric* a meaning – lies in the fact that for the first time in those six million years human society is in a position to provide the cure; by means of a salve capable of almost any acrobatic. Debarred for millennia from realizing his pipe-dreams by the need to scratch a subsistence from the soil sapiens-sapiens has at last succeeded in forging an instrument – high technology – through whose magic any future he dreams up for himself and his kind can be realized, except power over death. The New Jerusalem for instance. Always a key objective in the thoughts of this dissatisfied animal, its conquest now depends – no longer on poverty of means – on poverty of ideas. As the Americans say the problem for presidents today is not how to wrestle with the future but how to choose what future to wrestle with.

Our own post-prandial pranksters decided long ago that there is only one future worth bothering about; the cult of the British

Constitution. To be consecrated at one Punk Festival after another in the name of parliamentary reform. What happens after you've solemnized those reforms and dismembered the Festivals no one seems to know or care. On both sides of the Atlantic the end-product is a vacuum we call freedom and know not what to do with. Yet an English parliament once sent out an army to capture the New Jerusalem and failed only because of Man's first Disobedience.

2

CRUDE APOCALYPTIC

Parousia

Utopia is not an English copyright, nor, come to that, a Christian one, though Christendom – the West – can claim to be the first genuine applicant for the patent. Ignoring the pastoral Utopias of Theocritus and Virgil and other classical ideas about the ideal world one can say that the messianic concept proper starts with Chapter vii of the Book of Daniel, the earliest Apocalypse, composed about 165 BC at the height of the Maccabaean revolt. It goes back, that is to say, beyond Christianity but not beyond Jewry. Understandable, this; the messianic convention is after all a Chosen-People gimmick. Stolen for re-use by whoever wrote the Revelation of St. John the Divine (AD 93), it then for the first time featured Jesus as the returning Saviour and King with whom the Saints would reign for a thousand years: the Millennium proper. Followed by the Resurrection of the Dead, the Last Judgment, and, by way of finale, the letting down of that august parachute, the New Jerusalem, from Heaven.

Thence onwards the New Jerusalem or Parousia or Second Coming was hourly expected by some group or other. By the Montanists in Phrygia, by Tertullian in Judaea, by Justin Martyr in Jerusalem itself, by eloquent Lactantius, by Commodianus, the inferior Latin Poet. Thereafter 'on earth' by Irenaeus, Bishop of Lyons, who, according to Dr. Cohn, did more than anyone to establish chiliasm* in the West.

Then the inevitable happened. Bored by its obstinate refusal to materialize 'on earth' somebody decided that Christ's *kingdom* was to be understood in a less bodily, a more heavenly, a more spiritual sense. Origen in the third century made the first move to discredit chiliasm by presenting *the kingdom* as an event that would

Chiliasm: the doctrine of the millennium: the view that Christ will reign in bodily presence on earth for a thousand years.

take place not in space or time but in the souls of believers. What stirred his profoundly Hellenic imagination, says Dr. Cohn,* was the prospect of spiritual progress begun in this world and continued in the next, a shift of interest eagerly taken up by the now organized Church. Thus in the fourth century when Christianity became the official religion of the Empire, ecclesiastical disapproval of chiliasm became 'emphatic'. Finally St. Augustine called the bluff of all remaining millennarists by insisting (in *The City of God*) that the book of Revelation must be understood as a spiritual allegory and the Millennium fully realized in the Catholic Church.

This became the Party Line. Irenaeus's chiliastic chapters were suppressed and in 431 the Council of Ephesus condemned belief in the Millennium as a superstitious aberration, liquidating thereafter the more militant of the Second Comers as (in the words of a later messiah, Joseph Salmon, the poetic Ranter) titillators of the flesh tumbling in the foaming surges of its own vanity.

The picture survived notwithstanding. Grew to enormous dimensions during the People's Crusades. And came to a head with the English Civil War, whose moving spirits introduced certain improvements into the design. Notably, for those who had just done away with one king, the doctrine that Christ, the other, would execute a psychic rather than material *instauratio* by slipping unobserved into the hearts of the new bosses (not just then burning to be demoted even by their Lord and Master) who thereupon became His Saints.

Government of the people by the Saints for the Saviour.

The Civil War

That as it happens was the last time Millennial slogans were rife throughout a whole community. Difficult though it is for us to believe the New Model and the City of London, besides the House of Commons, lived in hourly expectation of the establishment on English soil of this saintly kingdom. When on the noon of July 4, 1653, unbaring his soul to the newly assembled Parliament of Saints, the late Member for Cambridge grated out in his untuneable voice that the government of England was at the edge of the 'Promise and Prophecies', his words, mere verbiage for us, for him and his audience were fraught with tremendous – with apocalyptic – meaning. '*We are at the threshold,*' he cried, '*. . . why should we be afraid to say or think this may be the door to usher in the things that God has promised?*'

* *The Pursuit of the Millennium* by Norman Cohn (Secker & Warburg) p.13.

To which, on July 12, drunk with prophecy themselves and carried away by his own burning conviction, the Commons made reply by a declaration that 'as before the birth of Christ God's people were aware of the coming of a new world, so let England now be the instrument to complete the divine work by breaking the yoke and removing the burden of sin'.

Surprising words to issue from the portly bosoms of a hundred and twenty-nine (or thereabouts) MPs, but these sentiments were not claptrap; their authors believed they were saying something at once momentous and practical. So did the late Member for Cambridge. Calling up all the reserves of his secret strength this great man set himself the task of realizing in the flesh and substance of 'this world' what, with all their good intentions, his contemporaries were satisfied to do no more than make an ideal of for the next. *It was the destiny of the English, as he believed, to bring in a New Order which would revolutionize the political, social and economic history of mankind.*

Nor, though the greatest and most practical, was he the only Englishman with this faith. Not much more than four lifetimes ago a whole race of realists wrought and fought for the Millennium in the confident expectation of its instant materialization. They even brought the navy up-to-date and enlarged it (ten times) to secure the High Seas for, as they said, the coming of Christ. Odd isn't it, that except in terms of fossil energy or hydro-electrics or space travel the whole conception of a New Deal for man should have vanished out of mind as though it had never been – platform, pulpit, classroom, textbook, all innocent of any impulse even to record much less acclaim the great events of the seventeenth century, written off for practical purposes as a misfire.

A misfire some of them were, but on a level very different from that supposed by those who represent the business as some tedious wrangle between Parliament and Crown or Court and gentry or absolutism and democracy or commerce and feudalism or protestantism and popery or Anglicans and dissenters or Presbyterians and Independents, with, as a side-kick a horror-comic surrounding the removal of that bauble. Using soldiers to whisk away the Mace . . . pulling down Mr. Speaker . . . kicking out the Members . . . rather shocking, what?

Well yes, it was rather shocking, but how small a jolt beside the big one the bystander has coming to him at finding the vision of the great millennarists either misrepresented or blandly ignored. Since we who see so little are clear enough about one thing, that unless a New Order of a sort can be realized there isn't likely to be order of any sort to worry about, new or old, the matter seems worth looking into further; and when one does, one finds no misunderstandings more gross than those which have coagulated round the Civil War. The war that gave birth to the modern world and also to the man Hugo called the first modern man, that momentous figure who reversed the nation's destinies and later bestrode, colossus-like, the age.

Hearty Hamlet

Besides the voice this character had other unlovely qualities. He was incalculable, specious, violent. He had warts; he had a large copper nose; he suffered from verbal diarrhoea; he preached crude apocalyptic; he gave currency to much biblical cant; to top it all he had Welsh ancestors and a grandfather known to his contemporaries as Morgan ap William. Incorruptible, honest, humble and musical his name has become synonymous with Pharisaism. And Philistinism. Great he may have been, even in the Carlylean sense a hero, but far from nice in any nice sense of the word nice – so little nice that the British have always been undecided whether to give him a place in the hall of fame. No, reluctant rather than undecided; reluctant to accept either his stature or his achievement. Others have held him in a very different esteem; hardly one of the great European romantics but started his literary career with a bad play about the Protector. We still don't like him. Had Shakespeare lived to (say) Bernard Shaw's age to make him the last and greatest figure in what Goethe called the national epic, we might have taken another view. Shakespeare, however, gave up the ghost in Stratford the day this young man was entering his name as a gentleman commoner at Sidney Sussex College, Cambridge. A typical hearty much given to horse-play, rude noises and sudden furies, whose family name had not long been changed to Cromwell in compliment to another less towering but still great kinsman, Thomas of that ilk, the eighth Henry's Jack of all trades.

The issue would seem simpler had Oliver been a less complex character. Like that of so many bluff Englishman his pose as a homespun country gentleman was a mere surface affectation, almost a deceit. As an undergraduate at Cambridge he belonged to the ragsters and games players,* but his team-mates soon discovered in this burly chap qualities foreign to the football field

*Football and golf, James I's favourite games, were already occupying the thoughts of the D-kids.

and come to that, the altar rail. A character of many contradictions, fate played an odder trick than either knew when on the day she withdrew the Bard of Stratford from circulation the squire of Ely popped up in search of his destiny. As though as his creator passed away the greatest of Shakespearian creations had stolen back to Elsinore in disguise to take over the controls and so demonstrate how destiny would have handled Denmark's heir had that princeling failed to get in the way of a lethal weapon.

An all but impenetrable disguise, agreed, the blunt, broad, ruddy, warty, country squire with the big nose described as 'luminous' two centuries before Lear . . . and yet . . . isn't there something amazingly familiar about it all, the groans, the moans, the mutterings, the sudden startling transitions, action into inaction, prankster into hypochondriac, extra- into introvert, the public ink-throwings, private gnashings of teeth, breast beatings, broodings – even the stage soliloquies uttered in whispers that could be over-heard across a continent. Surely an outstanding example of nature imitating art; only seventeen years after, too, if the day referred to above be taken as the deadline. Until much later, when mistrust of his ambitions alienated friends as well as enemies. The Nose, as he was called, seems to have been regarded as the one fact of real worth in an ersatz world. Even later still, when in certain minds dark suspicions began to form of his intentions towards the Crown, they were dismissed by his familiars as unworthy of their subject.

For despite his contradictions this Hamlet lived to become a fully integrated human being who somehow reconciled the horse-coper (best judge of a horse in England) with the martyr to introspection, the Old Testament prophet with the noisy knock-about comedian – even in the face of battle 'he was naturally of such vivacity, hilarity and alacrity', wrote Richard Baxter, 'as another man is when he hath drunken a cup of wine too much' – the strategist, statesman and diplomatic double-dealer with the dashing cavalry soldier – 'in the field', his troopers said, 'the graciousest and most gallant man in the world'. Wild animal ferocity, remorseless puritanism, passionate magnanimity, a yearning for tolerance, a weakness for custard-pie – these were the other ingredients; and, various though they were, not one of them but was tested to the last sinew by the great events his massive nature precipitated and essayed to master.

Here the worst of the bizarre accidents that have conspired to falsify the Cromwellian legend makes its appearance. Because the stage upon which destiny chose to place this outsize character was by current standards small, the other actors British with a truly

British genius for underplaying their parts, and most of those who have since recorded the drama, whigs, tories or social realists, it has been taken for granted that what Clarendon called The Great Rebellion was a sort of miniscule French or American revolt. About as sane, this, as writing off the play mentioned above as bootless because Elsinore is remote and its prince marginal. Nothing could be sillier. Had it succeeded Cromwell's new deal would have rendered subsequent revolutionary history, German, American, French, and Russian, totally and absolutely redundant. In turn every one of their heresies went into the offensive; in turn Cromwell repulsed them; starting with the Establishment itself in the person of our Sovereign Lord the King. Thereafter, pulling out every known combination: the Church, the law, the reactionaries, the reds, the radicals, the rationalizers, the pragmatical fellows, the empiricists, the realists, the realpoliticians, the temporizers, the non-compromisers, the hot gospellers, the doctrinaire revolutionaries, the professional fanatics, the saved, the lost, the high tories (of whom he was one). Most heart-breaking of all, the pure in heart, who shared his objective albeit not his conviction how to achieve the goal – passionate idealists, like Harrison, who believed the forces of evil must yield to their unworldliness.

The Little Horn

Though he spurned their out-of-this-world statecraft Cromwell loved Harrison and the Fifth-Monarchy-Men better far than the Levellers with their inflexible republicanism. Neither a revolutionary nor a republican, not even a reformer – not even (as Maurice Ashley once suggested) a conservative reformer – he hated the reforming folly of those fellow-travellers to whom he had to represent himself as such when in fact his roots were deep in the countryside and its good earth, in the things of custom and convention, hunting, hawking, horses; in the slow organic development of human routines; in the memories of childhood; in loyalty to the Throne. A creature of habit, he could so little shed his early prejudices that even when in power he remained preoccupied with the Elizabethan enemy of his boyhood, Spain, turning upon the new dynastic ploys of France an angry but Nelsonian eye.

Why then did this high tory set the law at naught, frogmarch his sovereign to the scaffold, break Parliament and bring dictatorship to a land he risked his life times without number to make free of tyranny. Fill it with spies, secret police, fines, imprisonments, proclamations, penalties. In the words of the man of furious zeal for whom in accordance with the seventh chapter of Daniel the year 1660 was confidently expected to usher in the Fifth Monarchy – with Cromwell as the agent appointed by the Ancient of Days to inaugurate the Reign of the Saints – how came it that he should turn in the end into the Little Horn in the head of the Fourth Beast?

This is the problem. So long as Cromwell is made to pose as a great Parliamentarian fighting for the democratic ideal or a product of privilege fighting for the control of government by the parliamentary gentry, or a puritan fighting for freedom from 'flat Popery' the question is unanswerable. His actions become slightly more understandable when interpreted as the manoeuvres of an Independent fighting for freedom of conscience since it is arguable that a dictatorship which tolerated freedom of conscience (his did or anyway passionately tried to) was the only means in that day and age by which such could be achieved. Even so it isn't enough. So long as we persist, despite all Carlyle could do to rehabilitate it, in treating the puritan vocabulary as the language of humbug and double-talk and his and his buddies' religious tantrums as hysteria or hubris the mystery remains.

And here is where the historians, red, pink and true-blue, conspire with intentions totally honourable to falsify the issues of the Protectorate.

A strong word, conspire, unacceptable indeed insofar as it suggests pre-arranged winks and nods. Conspiracy, however, in the shape of an unspoken very-much-gentleman's agreement *not* to do or say certain things can take the negative form of dumb insolence, and this is exactly how some critics have chosen to act. Scepticism and determinism, natural selection and the laws of nature, inadmissibility of free will, venality of man – these weigh with them more than any claptrap about the puissance of the free and sovereign soul, an article they put no genuine faith in whatsoever.

As for all that damned hot air about sin, Christian liberty, Providence, revelation, Zion, grace, charity, while they would hardly send its prophets to the stake for ugly enthusiasm, how smugly do they echo the words of a Bull uttered by Innocent III at the Lateran Council of 1215 in condemnation of the impious Amaury, that fanatics of this type are not so much heretical as insane. Adding with Macaulay (after all they are a little liberal) but not insane enough to be put away.

Gentry Crisis

By corollary, since great affairs such as those we are discussing could hardly owe their birth to the quarrels of quasi-messiahs, other origins must be found, a crisis of the gentry, for instance, a 'rebellion of mutinous impoverished backward-looking provincial squires' who took up arms to resist the squeeze exerted on them by the Anglican Court and the monopolizing City, from both of which they were economically excluded, and both of which in their spleen they destroyed. Setting upon their ruins a brief, disastrous experiment – the republic of the gentry – with, as its figure-head, old Ironsides, a luminous-nosed declining squire.

By corollary again, the faiths they made such a nuisance of themselves about were hardly more than alternative (and fellow-travelling) ideologies, useful as a means of demonstration against the Anglican Court. Spleen, it would seem on this argument, is a more valid revolutionary instrument than revelation. Sinning coldly against the light and committing every kind of minor indignity upon the Holy Ghost, these sceptics still reject with contumely the Carlylean (and also the Weberian) view by presenting the greatest event in European history as a mere regrettable piece of bad temper by an indigent provincial squirearchy.

On no issue, admittedly, do the historians differ more widely. Seeing how greatly the social climate has changed since the seventeenth century it is hardly surprising if a discussion that was taken then on religious and moral grounds should have shifted now to constitutional and economic. And when so much puritan opposition to the monarchy had financial origins in capitalist greed; and when so much of the energies of the King who had a social policy of a sort were spent in protecting his country from the abuses this greed would bring, the temptation to side with Charles' Welfare State against the capitalist Commons is a pleasing one to be able to give way to. Many do, dismissing with appropriate words of regret the Protector (an enigma) and his Protectorate (an interregnum) as a blackleg phase in the otherwise dignified evolution of the British Constitution.

Suppose just for one instant this reading were wrong. Suppose our spine-chilling pessimism, the occupational disease of our century, were due to nothing more than a slight miscalculation, a minute error of judgment. Suppose this error, small though it be, had been introducing itself into all our calculations since. Suppose the seventeenth century, a time of social revolution and bitter feuds, of profound religious and ideological conflict, of a Europe divided into two camps – Protestant North, Catholic

South, and, as today, a German people torn in half between them – had more than the significance we allow it? Suppose history does repeat itself? Suppose the great issues at stake were not merely similar but identically the same, though neither constitutional nor (in the technical sense) religious, still less social or economic. Suppose that in popping the seventeenth-century question we were also popping the twentieth-century question? Suppose the answers we are usually given about Parliament and free institutions were poppycock. Suppose all this liberal business of democracy were not baby but baby's bathwater, scented, soft-soaped, murder to BO, albeit bathwater, not baby? Suppose, on top of all Cromwell tried to do to rescue this infant, baby *were* still mislaid, still crying in some airless cupboard in the hope of being found, released, picked up, comforted, petted, patted, pampered, plunged by all means in the bathwater of democracy and liberalism and majority rule and human rights and free institutions and parliamentary procedures, but done something else to as well – recognized – affirmed – acknowledged – given a name, a title, an estate, a right of citizenship, a right to *be*. Suppose the whole political history of the eighteenth and nineteenth centuries were discovered to be an elaborate side-kick.

Suppose – hold on to your seat-belt – the millennium remains still our proper goal and source of intoxication. Or if you prefer it, NU JU. Why not? Why not bring Jerusalem into line with modern notions of townscape and slam once for all the authorized version in its obstinate determination to present Utopia as a House of Correction where Serfs of the Spirit practise the Simple Life under inner compulsion from cracker mottoes (*work of each for weal of all*). Witness the most famous of all – Moore's – where without an official pass from the Local Authority the citizen wasn't even free to leave town. Compare this painful picture with Blake's, almost the only modern man to get a genuine kick out of the thing, who squarely stated and quite as clearly passionately believed that though green and pleasant England would never be the jolly place or Englishmen the slap-happy libertines of joy both would like to be until the NU JU was a reality. That the democratic machinery was invented for precisely this job his heirs have overlooked. They did at one time cast a hopeful eye on the US and while they did democracy and the NU JU showed signs of teaming up, but when the US went bad on them the thought of the slap-happy life seems to have faded out of political consciousness even as a pious dream.

Yet the fact that this machinery had a purpose and the fact

that this purpose, none other than to create a Parousia or Promised Land or New Dispensation or New Deal or New Jerusalem, after being adopted by the Church (which failed to realize it) was taken over lock, stock and barrel by the English Parliament – this matter of historic fact seems to be blandly ignored by all connected with our day, age, race, philosophy, economy, religion. And by a good many not so connected. The democratic instrument is there, groomed for the purpose, but the purpose itself has been mislaid. Accordingly, political history, not merely makes no sense but becomes almost impossible to describe so long as the efforts made by many kinds of people to create a new kind of man in a new kind of society go unrecorded. How can you begin to assess the dream without recognizing that its authors, the British, have always been inveterate, or un-regenerate, or perhaps one should say incurable, NU JUers? Before the Americans stole their birthright in puritanism and so rendered them frustrate the British were widely feared by the rest of Europe for their moral pretensions; nor until this century did the last grains of moral fervour desert them.

Moral fervour may not be an agreeable or even exemplary quality; we record its existence as a matter of history. The millennarist urge is the basis of English (moral) as opposed to French (rational) liberalism. In the seventeenth century it brought the moralists to the ultimate arbitrament of civil war.

Then vanished like Hamlet's Ghost. Retired, rather, wrapping its face in its cloak in that final act of defeat responsible for our chronic state of Angst today.

Perplexed Atlas

To be stuck down in a world packed with noises off, without the faintest clue what your values are; or, supposing them to be mis-laid, where to look for them, is a situation which has probably never occurred before in the six million odd years that offer records (of a sort) of man. A rum state of affairs, believe it or not – how rum contemporary men and women seem to be aware not at all. Rum it is, however, and never rummer than when in the extremity of their need the cause-sifters invent explanations of events ever progressively further from reality. The gentry crisis for example, to return to where we started. Without questioning the existence of such or the high authority of those who record it, one may fairly ask which, realistically speaking, has more significance for history, it or the manner of its exploitation by the puritan top brass. To put it another way, wide though the grounds of disagreement are on what the Civil War was about, one item does exist on which differences of opinion must surely be reduced to next to nothing, and that is Cromwell's opinion of what the Civil War was about. The bigger the vote for mere constitutional and legislative reform as an explanation the more redoubtably does the massive moral stature of Cromwell tower over the by comparison petty purposes of the other moving spirits of the time: in the words of his antagonist Lilburne, 'mighty and great, formidable and dreadful'; translating what might have been a mere squabble about gentry grievances to the cosmic plane of the Miltonic struggle.

For however he started out, long before the end Cromwell was almost entirely indifferent to any of the issues constitutional reform is expected to iron out, which explains one of the widely held misunderstandings about his behaviour. Entirely indifferent for example, so long as tolerance survived, to forms of government. As man or statesman, his whole energies were exercised to, as he said, 'roll yourself on God,' a means of locomotion as suitable in his view to the nation as to the individual. At many crucial moments he may have seemed, in C. V. Wedgwood's phrase, a perplexed Atlas, but there can, surely, be little doubt about what he, the 'most absolute single-hearted great man in England' (Lilburne again) was perplexed about. What the apostles of Reason deride as his disregard of logic, reformers his Blimpism, doctrinaire revolutionaries his dubious opportunism, and men of principle his chicanery, were all products of the vast indifference he felt for every talking point except the one quintessential issue that would change them all anyway: the New Look applied to Man. Jerusalem. Parousia. The moral Instauratio Magna; foundation, Christian liberty. Every action he took, even the mad-looking ones like that effort to incorporate the Dutch, the source of much derisive laughter at the time (actually a signal example of an extraordinary vision three centuries in advance of its day, aimed at consolidating a European Common Market of NU JUers) was dedicated with complete and singleminded devotion to this one objective.

Ignore this fact and as a historian you are reduced to treating the language of Zion as boloney and its authors as, again in the words of Macaulay referred to above describing the first Quaker, George Fox, indecent exhibitionists 'too much disordered for liberty and not sufficiently disordered for Bedlamm'.

You are dedicated, that is to say, to a falsification of the

29

drama of Christendom – or if you prefer it, the West – beside which the efforts of the Kremlin to rewrite history seem diffident, even timorous.

Forlorn Hope

Over the issue to which he gave first priority, Cromwell's fellow regicides, as he soon discovered, were no help. They could talk big; they couldn't act big. With their endless pedantries and prattlings he showed an extraordinary if smouldering patience. But when at last it became clear that under the Presbyterian yoke the revolutionary Parliament would be as little tolerant of unorthodoxy as the king and must bring to confusion all he had shed English blood to secure, of which freedom of conscience was the necessary prelude to a more comprehensive New Deal, he struck.

His course may not always have been so clear as these words suggest. What he did know with absolute clarity was that an opportunity to realize *The Kingdom* – Christ's – now offered, and seeing that he and he alone was in a position to be that territory's broody hen he took the dread decision only a hero could make to submit all to the issue even to the bitter edge of dictatorship and beyond. There was still an outside chance that the puritan revolution was indeed the instrument ordained by Providence to usher in the Thing that God had Promised.

A forlorn hope. Cromwell knew it at the last; Zion no more than the House of Commons can be wooed, and won by major generals, secret police. Before the end he was forced to face the fact that though his strait-waistcoat of law and order rendered the struggles of the old collapsing dispensation less frantic to itself as well as less deadly to the new infant the Civil War had spawned, it, the infant, was, by the parent who had gone through all the pangs of childbirth to give it life, unwanted.

The final cruel awakening, the discovery that men are too lightweight for their destiny. In his last years, broken with disillusion, he railed much against his own kind while the Parliament of Saints who in the last resort didn't really want it, or, come to that, him, stonewalled its way to victory over the Protector with the classic weapons of parliaments, obstruction, evasion, or as son Henry Cromwell put it, a tendency to be 'casual in its motions'. It being 'the natural genius of such great assemblies [Henry again] to be various, inconsistent and for the most part forward with their Superiors'. Henry 'wished Papa would consider this'.

His Highness did, and much else in that sort, notably, the fact that the nation at large as opposed to the bible belt wanted neither revolution nor uplift, nor the police-state of the Presbyters, nor the lawyers' hair-splittings, nor the Anabaptists' zeal, nor the Fifth Monarchists' mountebank Utopia, nor the Ranters' rant, nor – most wounding of all – the Lord Protector's Blakian Jerusalem. Exhausted and bored and sick of the whole bunch it just wanted to be left alone and said as much. Nor by any conceivable piece of Cromwellian double-think could the New Jerusalem be realized in such a temper or lack thereof.

Apprehending which he realized at last that there was no way to make men see that such parliamentary institutions, democratic conventions, universal brotherhoods, as are wished on society for its greater felicity and freedom are indeed, given one qualification, great and good things bringing in their train emancipation, progress, higher evolution.

Given one thing. Without that, nothing. Less than nothing. Worse than nothing. Anyway no better than bathwater.

Ingressio

Some historians, we still maintain, have totally misrepresented this aspect of the Cromwellian tragedy though not in a way to call in question their rectitude. Others in taking care to say it have done so with an excess of literary grace, designed to kill this sorry business with kindness as the only liberal, the only democratic, the only scholarly, the only gentlemanly, the only decent thing to do. No statement could be more liberal or elegant than that of the occasionally unliberal historian, John Buchan, when announcing 'Not since Caesar after Munda set about the re-ordering of the globe had a mortal will bent itself to so bold an enterprise' . . . yet the reference has a smug phrase-turning smell which succeeds very ingeniously in shelving the case by overstating it. To the phrase-turners the enterprise under discussion isn't a real issue, just the puritan paper tiger having a paper honeymoon, to be duly noted as they bustle forward to bring on the Merry Monarch and his blotting-paper tigress, the British Constitution, saved from O what an inky end. Memorable phrases; not something immanent in our business today. Our business today being occupied with the development of parliamentary or unparliamentary blotting paper, it's clear, isn't it that Cromwell not merely failed but erred, not merely erred but sinned, and sinned against the light.

Unjust perhaps to single out Buchan, a critic more understanding than some, who does maintain that he, Cromwell, failed in a greater task than establishing democracy; that the seventeenth century plumbed depths of human experience later centuries have neglected; that because his faith after his death went out of public view, indeed almost out of the memories of men, it did not therefore perish; that *The Kingdom* (which the puritans sought to realize) was an ingressio, the advent of a new thing.

Nevertheless, says Buchan, Cromwell 'wrought in a narrower field and influenced far less profoundly the destinies of mankind' than those cyclopean architects Caesar and Napoleon, and in the end 'left nothing that endured'. Hence England, after five systems of government tried out by the Lord Protector between 1653 and 1658, rejected, lock, stock and barrel, him, his tears, roarings of the spirit, sanctimonies, unctuosities, cajoleries, equivocations, protestations, prayers, perfidies, horseplay, consigning him and his to outer darkness (or anyway Huntingdon). Turned instead with a heartfelt sigh of relief to that other instauratio, the Restoration proper, and so 'blundered and sidled into modern parliamentarism', the system which combined expert administration with a measure of popular control – the True blotting-paper Cross.

There you have it, and you have it in Buchan in its most sympathetic form, the conscientious lip-service to puritanism of one who is a bit of a puritan himself, the effort to sound convincing, then the undisguised relief of a civilized man of affairs that the whole thing was a misfire. Demonstration on the one hand of a liberal capacity for understanding the other fellow's point of view even when it's the hottest of hot air; on the other the happy knowledge that it's going to be a resounding flop – what else could you expect a Jesus freak-out to be in the jungle of *Realpolitik?*

Thus while not exactly misrepresenting the facts the historian manages to falsify their significance and so impugns, totally without malice if not the good faith the good sense of the great puritan spirits. It could you will agree hardly be better put than by Buchan in his ingressio, advent of a new thing, yet look what in his eyes it all amounts to. He, Cromwell, 'plumbed depths of human experience which later centuries have neglected' yet 'left nothing that endured' so influenced the destinies of mankind 'far less profoundly' than those cyclopean architects C & N.

Why it follows that when you plumb depths of human experience from which others draw back nothing is left that endures isn't explained. The whole trouble springs from the biographer's first unspoken but implied assumption that the Reign of the Saints, the NU JU, was, au fond, a piece of hysteria that got what was coming to it.

Providence

The gigantic proportions this error has now assumed is revealed in the view, pretty well unanimously adopted by all his critics, of Cromwell's love affair with Providence, which dismisses as mere superstition 'the shocking assumption' in the words of that typical liberal historian Lord Morley, 'that little transient events are the true measure of the divine purpose' (which of course they are – what else could they be).* Thus do they deny at a stroke the one formula that makes sense of puritanism, in particular those providential signs he, Cromwell, perfected in order to turn himself on or off. The most significant of all his expedients, this, by his critics made to seem eccentric or even a bit mad, the goings on of a hot gospeller who without altogether taking leave of his senses has strayed so far down the road of superstition and fanaticism that men of prudent judgment draw back in something like dismay. As they would were some soothsayer to advise opening up the carcase of a convenient goat to establish how far the arrangement of the viscera bodes well for the 1980s.

True, Providence, the key to Cromwell's strategy, isn't easily distinguishable, from the mumbo-jumbo of augury and astrology dear to so many of the great captains from Alexander and the King of Cambodia onwards. Hence the accusations against him of blowing up impulses into Providential signals in order to identify his own obsessions with the will of the Deity. A temptation, agreed; flirtations with Providence do have their dangers. Yet in what is there not danger. And how anyway is one to accept the puritan – the Independent – attitude as being founded on a specific personal relation established between creator and creature without admitting also that this contract involves a personal interpretation by the latter of the revelations of the former. This was exactly what Cromwell brought to a fine art. The source of his massive inner strength lay precisely here, the vice-like grip on Providence and her signs and his talent for reading them, not by way of augury; not by the portents; not by the favourable disposition of the viscera – not by way of superstition – something

*There is a special providence in the fall of a sparrow – *Hamlet*.

better than that – wisdom justified of her children – things going right *because*.

Once insert that key in the lock and the mystery of his odd behaviour and vacillating policies vanishes. So do the ambiguities in his philosophy of action. Here lies the secret of all those locked doors, bloody chins, bouts of malaria or stone; also the interminable longeurs in his campaigns which so disconcert the historians. Doves no less than Hawks. The prophets of peace at any price still have enough of the old Adam to feel cheated when the man of the sword unexpectedly sheaths it. Nor does their irritation grow less when the reasons for his vacillations turn out to be indecision. Long, long were the inactions of this Atlas what time he awaited 'guidance'. Give him a sign and you would get the sudden fanatical ruthless stroke which consumed the obstacle, disintegrated the opponent. No sign, no action. Studying his hot and cold manoeuvres in this light one sees with what integrity the man of action nailed himself to his signs; not disdaining prevarication when the omens indicated that he must stall for time. Or submit to sanctions imposed against his own impatience by a mistress innocent of human impetuosity – Providence herself.

'Patience,' the Spanish proverb runs, 'and shuffle the cards.' And that was what he did. Time after time after time. It was Milton who most surely detected the titanic nature of Cromwell's private struggle; and wrote of it in moving words. 'He first acquired the government of himself, and over himself acquired the most signal victories, so that on the first day he took the field against the external enemy, he was a veteran in arms, consumately practised in the toils and exigencies of war.'

It was no less than the truth. From day to day of the Great Emergency Cromwell schooled himself to temper his impulses to one still small voice, the voice of Providence. Or – agony much worse, the absence thereof. A private self-denying ordinance signifying what indeed it was, a signal piece of self-mastery. The technique is illustrated in a tiny way by his foot-dragging tactics at the Putney Debates (October-November, 1647), which occupied all the army's energies, and cynosured the nation's eyes. Of the ardent new dealers who made up that strange military consortium, Cromwell let himself be counted amongst the fire-eaters who were thirsting to liquidate first the King, then the Lords, since, for his own part (as he said), he could see no future safety with either Lords or King.

No future safety for the NU JU, he meant. And that he meant what he said we have good reason to know; the monarch's

…ead did, later, roll at his, Cromwell's command, right into the basket. Yet if his peers expected to blackmail him into instant action as they did they were soon disabused. Not for a moment did The Nose mean to make a move until what a modern dictator would call historic necessity, or, as he put it, 'their' – Charles' and the Lords' – 'ungodliness' – Providence in other words –forced his hand.

Nor did he. In one of those nauseous harangues of his which so antagonize the modern reader he explained why. So far gone were these two parties, Charles and the Lords, in wickedness that God would probably destroy them anyway. Seeing which, why not leave the whole business to God and so avoid responsibility for the scandal. 'God can do it without necessitating us to a thing which is scandalous, and therefore let them that are of that mind wait upon God for such a way where the thing may be done without sin and without scandal too.'

Typical Cromwellian double-talk. On the surface Pharisaism could hardly go further. Yet the outcome showed that there was one high tory who meant exactly what he said even when he said it in words that strike as false as words can to a generation like ours which has no experience of the ear-to-Providence tactics of the student of the psychological moment. Addict of organic political evolution, iconoclast only by hard necessity, nothing even in a crisis would induce him to take action till 'events' – Charles' providential obsession with prevarication – eventually forced a move. His whole purpose was to bring action back into the line of valid organic development by subordinating personal impulse – his even more than the other thugs' – to historic necessity. Momentous decisions only when they become inevitable. Once get around to the theory of Providence, or as we should say the psychological moment, once perceive that the pause even more than the action was a vital part of the checking-up process; once accept Cromwell as Providence's champion checker-upper, then and only then do his tactics lose all taint of equivocation. All taint, too, of expediency with which this method is easily confused in the superficial twentieth-century mind. What parallel equally superficial there is between Cromwell and Napoleon is significant precisely because of the contradictions in their respective temperaments, failure to pin-point which accounts for the misrepresentations that dog the former's reputation to this hour. He was a Big or Little Corporal, not much doubt about that, he had the edge over other men, the masterful spirit, the genius, and the temptation to impose his will on his age.

The contradiction lies in his resistance to all these siren voices. A dictatorship he did admittedly create yet how poor, how piddling a thing. Anyone who considers Cromwell incapable of creating a more serious tyranny should ponder his actions in Ireland, the actions if not of a gorilla, a tiger, and not a paper one. This tiger created a sheepish dictatorship (of which he named himself, sheepishly, the shepherd); and for a reason exactly opposed to Napoleon's who assumed the purple to do precisely what Cromwell refused to do – impose his will on mankind. The Lord Protector imposed no will, neither his nor anyone else's. Prevaricated instead, temporized, toyed with the purple, sent the purple away, shut himself up, cut himself shaving, prayed, growled, gloomed, issued ordinances that effectively safeguarded the Commonwealth from his fellow-travellers, the dogmatic religionists, the doctrinaire revolutionaries, the sea green incorruptibles, the republicans, the egalitarians, the men of principle, the men of reason.

But above all, from that most puissant potential threat to the State – the Lord Protector. A dictatorship unworthy of the name, the Protectorate turns out in the last analysis to be nothing less than the sign of his own rejection of the Lord Protector's towering ambition to realize the NU JU. *Not* to impose his own will on the world, on the contrary to hold it in abeyance, together with the wills of his peers – for such a totally negative purpose was this dictatorship established; in the faith, or hope (premature as it happened) that a mastermind was working within the age and the belief that neither they nor he must oppose or put obstacles in the way by pride of reason or person.

Bad Samaritan

There was – or there wasn't. Providence or nothing. An heroic either/or, well named interregnum. The Protectorate was a vacuum, a huge vacuum, created by the Protector against, amongst other things, his own high wind. Designed to force himself in company with crew and passengers to wait on Providence, than which no lesser gale must be permitted to fill the sails of the Ship of State over whose destiny he saw himself as something even inferior to a shepherd, an officer standing a watch; and a junior one at that (his own figure was a constable keeping order in a village).

If the winds blew, the sails didn't fill, and at the end Cromwell joined Plato in thinking men unworthy of their destiny. The vacuum remained a vacuum. Into which in due course poured those other lightweight breezes, those pouter-pigeon puffs, more suited to the barque and the calibre of the crew.

Poured in, caught the ship of State and blew it complacently back into the port whence it had once set out for the promised land. Mayflower into Skylark: the round trip. A glorious return, productive of much junketing and wassailing. And in the end, by the inverted standards of human progress, a big success for the Social Body, busied like Martha, about the disembarking of many delightful people and unloading of rich cargoes.

Yet if Buchan was right in saying that Cromwell failed to affect the destinies of mankind does it follow that he achieved nothing. In that sense, since he too has been consistently fooled, Christ achieved nothing.

Of course Cromwell failed, and with his fall the nation relapsed into its Old-Adamic self. A failure sure enough but not his, the nation's. Man's. He could do little more than lay down the framework for the new dispensation and that framework stays down, merely awaiting the moment we decide to use it. Failure on that scale is hardly nothing. Over the immediate issue his conviction that Christ or anyway his *kingdom* would pop up, when for reasons we now understand better than he Christ wasn't playing or couldn't play, was cheated. In the greater perspective he was triumphantly right.

Of course he failed. And here at last we come to the gravamen of the charge against democracy and the twentieth century, because sooner or later by one bomb or another we shall have to bring ourselves to face the unpleasant fact that that failure – the misfire of Cromwell's NU JU – is the source of our present disarray. Naturally enough we do what we can to forget the message if not the man but sooner or later events will catch up on us and bring him back into current usage. A man who because his own dream was born out of due season, forcing him in moments of the State's supreme danger to break his own rule of conduct by surrender to the seduction of action or in the case of Ireland the self-delusion of the avenger, did, notwithstanding, set out to achieve what no other single one of the great captains has even conceived, let alone essayed to do.

Of course he failed. Overshooting the Promised Land he fell on his face in the desert where like any other mirage the Millennium evanesced. Christ was still around but passed by on the other side, eyes averted. Providence cleared her throat and looked away too. As he died the world pulled the curtains on another loser.

3

INSTAURATIO MAGNA

Revelation and Reason

This should have been the end of the saga. It wasn't. Something startling had happened. Even before Cromwell's own suspicions that she had jilted him were aroused, his mistress, Providence's averted eyes had fallen on an alternative programme and liked it. Suppose we look at the situation again as those eyes may well have seen it. The Tudors, arguably the most successful tyrants of all time, by relieving the English with no clear intention of every dictatorship but their own, then throwing the royal weight against the old and behind the new learning, had released amongst their newly liberated subjects a young wine-lake of controversy and polemic.

Well . . . not all their subjects. The lower orders would have to wait another century before Selina, Countess of Huntingdon, known to her husband, the ninth Earl, as Old Goody, saw fit to endow them with Wesley and indubitable souls. In seventeenth-century society – apart from the theologically enlightened Other Ranks of the New Model – an awareness of one's soul was the prerogative of the nobility and gentry; amongst whom the most vocal were the intemperate parliamentary squirearchy of the House of Commons, by the defeat of Popery endowed with a new and intoxicating power. Nothing less than an audience of the Deity *without benefit of clergy*: a personal hot-line to God. Hard though it now is to believe, the gentry of England went through the roof at the mere idea of this sensational confrontation. The Scriptures became their Encyclopaedia Britannica and the celebrations took the form of a bottle party, ending like so many other bottle parties in fisticuffs which came to a head with the drunken brawl of the Civil War. Not the first of England's civil wars but unique amongst all wars in being used by the victors – aptly enough seeing that it was his bread and wine they were drunk on – to write Christ and His

Kingdom, the Millennium, into the peace treaty. An impressive – bizarre indeed – use of a winning streak; though as Providence knew if no one else did unrealizable in that day and age even by a man of the stature of Cromwell. Hence her currently more eligible diversion. Hence an amendment to the above which ought to read not 'came to a head', but 'came to two heads', both intoxicated, the first pie-eyed on the promise of the individual's personal contact with his Maker (the bible-bashers); the second paralytic on the heady liquor of the *Instauratio Magna* (the Natural philosophers).

For by the middle of the century another prophet – almost another messiah – had taken up the running; none other than the parent of the *Novum Organum* who to Providence's obvious satisfaction was already offering an alternative route to the Deity by way of his, the Deity's, own work, *the Creation*. And Providence liked it a lot. Enough, indeed, to buy outright the Baconian dream, presented for all to see in *The Advancement of Learning*. There in 1626 the groundwork for a scientific credo was for the first time laid down in the *Cogitata et visa* which had set out to revalidate the gospel of nature – or, as its author would say, the *True Philosophy* – after the long medieval embargo. Even had he guessed how the ball was bouncing Cromwell would hardly have considered himself double-faulted since the advancement of learning was one of his aims; yet in the outcome the event precipitated his defeat.

Providence, however, could only back her own hunches. The exchange of a viable for an unviable objective would in the view of that roving eye be no more than an act of justice. As for Oliver's cause, a century or two, or three – almost overnight by her standards – would see it coming up for review, so of guilt she felt almost none at all. Shifted her patronage instead, not even troubling to disabuse him, to a likelier lad, Francis Bacon, and dead-pan as ever used the interregnum Oliver, the old love, had engineered to rear another family of ideas, on the principle that his purpose would be served in the end. A sound, indeed Providence's only working principle, the one great issue on which she disagrees with man.

The fact was, Bacon's scientific offensive had been jumping all sorts of guns since the 1620s and now with a general advance on all fronts the specialists seeing an opportunity to take over the revolution made a bid to do so. An inspired move, in the eyes of the natural philosophers, but surprisingly enough the bible-bashers took to it too, in virtue of the opportunity the situation offered for another reconciliation they were burning to achieve

– that between – not merely the Creator and His creatures – between His creatures and the Creation – *Nature* – contact with which man had (according to the Church) been jockeyed out of at the Fall. Christ's kingdom, that is to say, could now as ever be approached by way of revelation; but under the new management it could also be wooed by way of the Creator's own methods of work in the physical world, now at long last by the Deity made re-available under a new edict that found reason (or as we should say science) no longer a dirty word. No longer the adversary of revelation. A sign that he, man, by the pursuit of natural philosophy, was now to be permitted to re-enter the circle of Eden.

Terrible nonsense, needless to say. According to Genesis man had been banished from Eden for exactly that offence, becoming too knowing for the comfort of the Deity, who was getting anxious about his own position as top person; a wily way of describing the transition from the instinctual to the self-conscious animal. Not that it mattered at this particular juncture what interpretation was put on the Fall; the fascinating thing is that for a brief moment under the Commonwealth religion and science were joined in holy matrimony; creating in the loaded emotional state of the day that extraordinary episode whereby executive and legislature were brought to conceive that it might be possible to create a world with a novel life-style – Jerusalem – under the new management of Christ Scientist. To say by way of verdict as some historians do that the net results of all this fanfaronade were certain matters of constitutional reform will seem unbelievable to future critics. For the puritan scientists, already more numerous during the Commonwealth than either earlier or later in that century, Bacon's *Instauratio Magna* became as Charles Webster* says, almost a rival to the scriptures, culminating under the next Instauratio (of Charles Stuart) in the salons of the Royal Society and the sibylline graffiti of oracle Newton.

For these wonders the puritan revolutionaries can take, not all, but a good deal of the credit. Though shattered by the Thirty Years' War the Continent went on producing ideas and thinkers, and some of the new-born savants made the Commonwealth their home from home (Comenius and Hartlib, for example, the second of whom settled in England for good). Any road, it was a tearaway success. In a twinkling the world God made in six days, resting

*Charles Webster: *The Great Instauration: Science, Medicine and Reform, 1626-1660* (Duckworth).

the seventh, was transformed into the mechanist Newtonian universe, where, led by astronomy, all phenomena shed their metaphysical presuppositions. So complete was the Baconian triumph that revelation of the old orthodox kind began, maybe, to seem a bit *vieux jeu;* and, as such, could be handed back to Church, State and Crown, who could likewise be handed back. Which some would hold was just about what Charles II's Restoration amounted to, a curtain wall of orthodoxy pulled over the steel frame of the new scientific Jerusalem under whose audacious structure the Royal Society and the new (in our parlance classical or Newtonian) physics were happy to find a partnership with religion.

Not all their contemporaries were so pleased. The nation itself was less in love than its leaders with either the Baconian oeuvre or that other Kingdom and its King, Christ; preferring rather the Merry Monarch and *his* kingdom in an instauratio its fans describe as a return to sanity after a disastrous flirtation with paranoia.

Creep

THE IMPROVIDENT SOCIETY

A petty sneaking thief I knew –
O Mr. Cr——, how do you do?

William Blake

4

CHRISTIAN LIBERTY
AND CHRISTIAN LIBERTINISM

Demystification of Revelation

That final Restoration, Charles Stuart's, did at least rehabilitate
one great institution, the Church. As soon as *anglicana* could be
added by way of qualification to *Ecclesia* the claim could be
made by the Laudians – and was – that freed from medieval
papistry and its malpractices the English Church would now
return to the purer tradition of its founder, St. Augustine of
Canterbury. Whose disciplines while strict did, by apostolic succession from the Early Fathers, provide escape from later bonds
and worse, be they popish or protestant. A kind of freedom also
under two tremendous concepts, Christian poverty – the challenge
to scarcity – and Christian liberty, based on its founder's
remarkable axiom that in my service is perfect freedom. The first,
except amongst those who donned habit, wimple or soutane,
never had less than a hard time getting off the ground; the second
hit the jackpot with the puritan revolution, thereafter degenerating
into practices so little agreeable to its guardians, the clergy, that
had the in-word not by now become toleration its addicts might
well have faced that earlier deterrent, the stake.

Under the Commonwealth no question of that. What was, or
rather *now is*, in question touches as we have seen on the strange
– one can perhaps say unique – alliance of reason and revelation,
law and Christian liberty, science and Christ's Kingdom, Nature
and the NU JU. Unexpected running mates at any time, whose
partnership in that day and age prompts the student in view of
their obvious rivalry in ours to ask himself how such a hostile duo
could ever have gone in harness together. For they did; and this
by one guess or another brings the debate right back to the point
where it started, the great talking point of the day in its liberating
if not Christianizing role: Christian liberty itself.

Christian liberty, observe. Not abstract liberty. Liberty with a tiger in its tank. Before it can even get onto the page the abstraction *freedom* is qualified by a notion which makes process of principle, dynamics of mechanics, a mobile of a stabile. One may have no use for Christianity and still see that the men who coined this phrase knew better what they were about than the doctrinaire revolutionairies of the First Republic or the human-rights drearies of our own, for both of whom the ultimate good consists in that abstract liberty of which D. H. Lawrence said: 'What could be more hopelessly uninteresting.' This liberty wasn't abstract, a mere principle, but the consequence of throwing the onus on a higher justiciary than that of the police court – what Camus meant presumably in saying perfect liberty makes a nonsense of the law (adding, perfect law makes a nonsense of liberty). Tempting in this context to speculate whether perhaps the catalyst may after all have been exactly this higher authority or morality; demanding of science a striptease exposing the Deity's works – yes – but something more, the means by which *revelation*, in the orthodox meaning of the word, might itself be de-mystified. What else is physics than an essay in that kind of demystification, Christian or not, a revelation for sure; and also, as they felt in the Middle Ages, a pretty damned liberty. One might go even further by raising another debatable question: whether or not the notion of Christian liberty was more responsible for the puritan revolution than the puritan revolution for the notion of Christian liberty. However that may be its greater spirits were beyond doubt moved to see the blueprint for Zion as embracing both ideals, religion inevitably, but also the Great Instauration or rebirth of knowledge by means of which man would regain his dominion over nature and so his rapprochment with the Lord God; and so in the process realize Christ's Kingdom on earth. The Millennium.

Christian Liberty

As a higher morality, dead, and as a political concept not merely dead but buried, the notion of Christian liberty could seem hardly worth pursuing in any modern context. Yet in its wider implications the concept is crucial to much more than the understanding of the Civil War, the problem of our own liberties, our own democracy, our own future, the future of the West itself. As a political idea, that is – religious revivalism is not the subject of this discussion. Debated in endless detail by the theorists of the Protectorate it became an important part of the current jargon;

in the end indeed a nauseating kind of cant. For everywhere the New Dealers met – in the ranks of the army, in the lobbies of the House of Commons, in barracks, camps, clubs and pubs – plain English was stretched to its limits and often beyond to develop political conceptions – Christian liberty was a *political* conception –that have yet to enter the consciousness of twentieth-century man. Arguments which never before leaped the monastery wall or escaped the clutches of the cinerary urn were bandied about between tough fighting men who treated them as a good deal more politically absorbing than Social Security or Nationalization or VAT or the standard rate of income tax.

Nor was the discussion confined to the low-browed evangelists. Domes at least as lofty as Milton's made contributions of consequence to a debate which still remains unsolved, if only because its very name and substance has gone out of meaning and memory. While accepting the rational as well as the Christian solution to every political question and thus by inference admitting man to have duties legal as well as moral, and liberties civil as well as religious, Milton maintained that the one completed the other. Christian liberty, in short, complemented, enhanced, enlarged, fulfilled the civil code by incorporating it within a geater rationale. By, that is, accepting reason not superstition as the basis of the religious impulse: the higher reason.

Thus at a single stroke he solved, as he maintained, the old headache of religious versus civil authority which had foxed Luther and pretty well everyone else. On these grounds he based his own anarchist argument for universal toleration, religious and civil, maintaining with other free spirits of the Commonwealth that a resolution of all problems, legal as well as spiritual, lay in a society whose liberties were unlimited, inasmuch as its Christian character fulfilled the law by invoking a higher one, an easier, a more rewarding order, defined tactfully enough in King James' Version as charity.

After that, only one outstanding question remained. Is normal society prepared, is it morally equipped, to act at so lofty a level? Upon this issue hinged many of the tergiversations of the Lord Protector. Because, while Christian liberty did become the slogan of all who could conceive of the law as being operative at a higher level than the police court (whose authority Parliament is), this level, as its backers had to admit, was pretty stratospheric. The burning question thus became, who could be trusted to operate at that great height. Which brought from the hot gospellers, the Millennarists, the answer they had been waiting to give since the war began – none but the Saved, the Saints, the Elect of Calvinist doctrine, groomed by grace before time began for precisely this job. A new élite of prigs who in the delightful business of dragooning the non-elect would make of Parliament their own Sanhedrin of 70, backed by their own sanctimonious cops and saintly stool-pigeons.

That was the point at which the barrack-room lawyers among the Levellers stepped in, men who could smell dictatorship by élites a mile off. Wasn't this just one more despotism? A new threat to liberty in the name of liberty? Wasn't new Fifth Monarchist like New Presbyter old priest writ large?

They were right of course. No question about it. Here was a new threat to doctrinaire equality, one that must be smashed. And smashed it was, by the simple device of reversing Milton's argument; separating, as the lawyers put it, the order of Grace from the order of Nature. After all, if none but prigs could be expected to step up their behaviour to the standards of Christian liberty – the order of Grace – there were other standards even the unredeemed could recognize, to wit, the lower as against the higher reason. From the novel assumption that no distinction could be made between revelation and reason they reneged by insisting, rightly from one point of view – and let us hasten to add with the aim of safeguarding spiritual as well as political freedom – that the distinction *must* be made. Right down to its ultimate outcome in the *de facto* segregation of Church and State. For one the moral, for the other the civil code; a solution which has remained in force from that day to this, with everything to recommend it except the trifling circumstance that it sidesteps the whole issue. It sidesteps the whole issue in postponing the only thing that *is* at issue, the 'fulfilling' of the Mosaic by the Christian law; the abdication, that is, of civil in favour of Christian liberty; of the police court by the private conscience; of 'this world' by the no-longer 'next'.

Christian liberty, however, as one can see, was asking a bit more in the context of the 1640s and 50s than any of the actors in the drama, including Cromwell, could stomach. After all their heads would soon be underneath their arms should the other side acquire the liberty without the Christianity, so all too suddenly the Saintly rule collapsed. On top of the Fifth Monarchists; on top too of those members of the centre party, Cromwell amongst them, who were temperamental fellow-travellers. Collapsed so far as to frustrate the real potential of the revolution and reduce old copper nose himself to the state of gibbering impotence in which he imposed his stand-still on the nation.

Collapsed with so final a flop and into such oblivion that even Professor Wodehouse, whose introduction to *Puritanism and Liberty* debates these very points, sees nothing inconsistent in adding: 'from the vantage point of a later century no one will doubt that the most important political document to emerge from the revolution was one temporarily defeated but destined to ultimate triumph, the sovereignty of Parliament.' No liberty higher than the order of Demos occupies it seems the thoughts even of a Wodehouse. All the revolution boils down to in the end is constitutional reform meaning parliamentary evolution. And of course it was easy enough for doctrinaire and legalistic republicans who held by Reason and the Rights-of-Man to make fools of the heady optimists who thought in terms of the 'perfect liberty' of the Christian dream. Yet properly understood (as Cromwell and Milton understood it) Christian liberty sails as high above human rights as human rights rise above slavery. Is in fact the only stuff capable of sustaining the 'earthly majistracy' in which Society's New Deal must, in the words of a noble sermon preached by Thomas Collier at the Putney Debates on September 29, 1647, be invested. Don't make the mistake, he says in effect, of thinking the NU JU can wait for the next world. Heaven is inside you. To realize it on earth you have to do no more than follow the impulses of your real (not false) self. 'We have had and still have exceedingly low and carnal thoughts of heaven, looking on it as a glorious place above the firmament out of sight and not to be enjoyed till after this life.' Forget, he exhorts his audience, that place up there in the clouds; bring your heavenly business down to earth; realize it now. To realize the heavenly – that is the *real* –business of life – *now* – is the true object of man.

The dream faded. Sooner or later, however, and probably sooner than later, we shall have to bring it out of cold storage and try again. In the seventeenth century it brought fine radical minds to the realization, as we have said, that science itself was a new aspect of revelation and could almost be regarded as a demystification of the old. No need, as we have said, to give the English puritans the sole credit for a movement that was wide-spread in Europe. But their unique influence on events may be seen surely enough in the slant they gave to the scientific offensive, particularly in their preference for the development of agriculture, horticulture, metallurgy and communications, creating a new field of industrial employment and thus work for the 'deserving poor'. Hence capitalism. Hence eventually the industrial *revelation*; in which light the puritan momentum may be seen as far from exhausted after three hundred years.

Seen thus the idea that it fizzled out in parliamentary reform seems very odd. So does the dismissive approach of the modern Englishman to the great puritan radicals in view of his own attitude to current ills, which might be described as – to put it mildly – unheroic. Craven would also describe it. Abject is another good word.

The Antinomian Heresy

How abject we can deduce from the later fate of Christian liberty itself, known to the Church in its palmy days as the Doctrine of the Free Spirit. This left a soul well and truly washed in the Blood of the Lamb free of both customary and civil law and thus at liberty in theory anyway to gratify every possible peccadillo from romance to rape, roulette to robbery. Provided always the action was carried out in the name of Christ. This was the heresy the Ranters sought to revive, not without success. One can't say it flourished exactly, so many of its exponents having been eliminated in cleansing fires, nevertheless it had gone on obstinately going on, giving sleepless nights to the Holy Office ever since Tanchelm hawked his bathwater. The strategy is simple enough, though practised widely in ignorance of its guile by addicts not as yet wised up on the alliance (or misalliance) of sensation and emotion; between which popular opinion still hardly distinguishes. When both are in contention it's quite usual to invert the order of their going, for the perfectly *sensible* reason that in general we aren't in command of our emotions, while the senses can be harnessed for action by many well-established means. Booze, one of the popular sources of revelation; or porn, the inspiration of many acts of love. Or incense, liberator of the religious impulse. Thus Marguarite de Hainault: who in 1310 was liquidated by the Inquisition for maintaining that the soul absorbed in Divine Love could yield without sin or remorse to the desires of the flesh. This or its converse – that surrender to the desires of the flesh may induce the soul to cultivate a taste for divine love – has found backers amongst the Faithful from the thirteenth century Brethren and Sisters of the Free Spirit, whose founder, Almeric, like Marguarite taught that the sins of the flesh if done through the love of God were absolutely okay, right up to the Ranters of Cromwellian England. Or the Muckers of Königsberg. Or the fans of Henry Prince at his Agepemone in Somerset. Or – in the Paris of the 1830s – the followers of the prophet Mapah, a portmanteau god whose name

(Mamman and Papa joined in a new and holier matrimony) signified the bisexual nature of the Deity.

No doubt about it, this, the famed antinomian heresy which holds a Christian under the influence of Grace to be emancipated from the ties of conventional morality sprang straight from the loins of Christian liberty. Legitimately born it would seem at first sight; in the outcome an indubitable bastard, somersaulting the philosophy in ways that gave it a very different slant. Those lucky souls who were well and truly dipped in the Blood of the Lamb found themselves free suddenly to proposition revelation by way of carnal practices. Christian libertinism it might be called, the historic inversion which came to be known in the USA of the nineteenth century as Baptism by the Holy Spirit. In short, the physical thrill; in its lowest contemporary form, the fix – turn-on – get loaded – drop out – but at a more responsible level the urge to make contact with reality – the Promised Land – by geeing up the physical sensibilities in ways custom has agreed to regard as unlawful, or at least unconventional. Freedom and opportunity made the US the perfect theatre for such skylarks, with sex the normal if not the inevitable fermenting agent. There were those who deploring the carnality as much as the duality developed a suspicion of one principal or the other, generally the female; hence of woman as the prime source of the divisions within mankind. Hence of marriage, hardening in some cases into the cult of celibacy. The separatists were at the start anyway celibate and the Amani Society viewed women with grave suspicion. Anna Lee of Manchester, England, suspected men, on the other hand; and after doing time for 'the violent manifestation of her religious fervour', dismissed her husband on the ground that the cause of the Fall was the sin of sexual intercourse. One might expect him to have been slightly miffed, but, admirable man, without a word said in anger or even sorrow, he instantly enrolled as a disciple and followed her to the USA whither she decided to emigrate with the rest of her company of Shakers, that saintly but eccentric band. Of whom there were soon some five thousand executing the ritual dances peculiar to the sorority, meek, industrious, celibate, and since they would not make them, adopting children to enlarge the community.

Stirpiculture

However most of those who were exercised about the Ma and Pa within us were more interested to bring them together than keep them apart. Lucinia Umphreville for one, the popular-izer of Spiritual Marriage and founder of a practice with which her name should be imperishably coupled: holy kissing. Less subtle, Mary Lincoln of Brimfield, Mass, and girl friends took to darting at midnight into the bedrooms of young preachers to compromise themselves in the eyes of the earth-bound, and, better still, secure the physical thrill which as we have seen became the standard method of obtaining Baptism by the Holy Spirit.

This was bundling, a word with many English regional associa-tions, very celebrated in its day. Mary's own activities were brought to an end only when she and her friends disrobed and bundled– or, as we should say, streaked – through Massachusetts leaving their wardrobe behind them. Holy Kissing, however, survived; oddly enough as a form of mortification; gaining virtue in proportion as it was practised upon men whom it was a 'trial' to kiss. Later cults of the mid-nineteenth century went further and fared not worse, until in the course of nature they arrived at what the celebrated evangelist John Humphrey Noyes described with exquisite delicacy as the 'negative theory of chastity'. This remarkable man of extraordinary piety introduced into his community at Oneida, New York (whither his sect, the Perfection-ists, moved in 1847) an institution called complex marriage – wife-swapping, no less – object, to by-pass the possessive property-owning habit of mind one party to an orthodox marriage acquires for the other; known to the Oneida community as selfish love. To guard against this character-fault Noyes, when one of his lady members became enceinte, would demand that the father-to-be should surrender the mother-to-be to another.

No attempt was made to solicit the lady's views, possibly on the principle that for a wife any change is a change for the better. For the husband it wasn't always so easy, in the case of a young man called Charles not easy at all. Poised to become a father in consequence, as Dr. Noyes sonorously put it, 'of what we call Stirpiculture', Charles was perturbed at the idea of a swop and it was only after a severe struggle, for he adored the girl, that he was moved to let another Perfectionist share his wife's pillow. An act of self-denial by which Charles acquired in the eyes of Mr. Noyes such merit for his success in overcoming mere animal instinct that he became a model for the whole community. And marital general post did it seems work extraordinarily well for 30 years; the love-ins at Oneida seem to have created a state of social and married bliss shared by few counterparts in the dreary monogamic world outside its gates.•Indeed the community was celebrated for its homogeneity and good temper right up to 1879 when clerical persecution by the Presbyterian Synod of Central New York led to the holding of a Special Convention at Syracuse, where Noyes, by then an old man, was prevailed on not to persist with Complex Marriage in the face of the annoyance its raging success had caused. Stirpiculture went on – when does Stirpiculture not go on – but under the official banner of monogamy. Not long after, the community broke up, though whether as a result of the ban or the death of the founder which happened about the same time is anyone's guess.

Ours is that Complex Marriage was, like Salt Lake City's, a piece of political rather than religious planning. The keying up of Oneida's love life, though it may have helped to keep the Perfectionists in the kind of emotional state favourable to red-hot Revivalism, acted first perhaps as an incentive not to quit the party.

A still more complex marriage pattern was built into the gospel of counterparts borrowed from Swedenborg via our old friend the Seer of Poughkeepsie by Thomas Lake Harris, the fascinating founder of the Brotherhood of the New Life. Bearded, violent, he inhabited Brocton, Salem on Erie, and shared the Shakers' and Mapah's belief that God was a bi-sexual creature, but thereafter parted from them on vital issues.

Seeing that he is made in God's image, man, he argued, must seek to imitate the Supreme Being by making one with himself any member of the sex who shows promise of being his true counterpart. On earth however this charmer's parts could easily be distributed throughout the whole sex. Accordingly, unless you were pretty spry you might mislay her in mislaying her parts, so the thing to do was to keep a sharp lookout, divided as your counterpart might be amongst a whole gaggle of girl friends. Wherever you came on a chip as it were of the old or rather the young block you were expected to woo and of course win the chip; so making good one more small gap in the jigsaw of the celestial female.

'Father', as he was known to his flock, had a block or counterpart very much his own, a heavenly floozie called Lily Queen, non-existent in the flesh but destined through the mouth of Father to give the new revelation to the world. And through the mouth of Father Lily Queen let it be known that any nice girl who made the right approach via the bed-chamber of Mr. Harris would never regret it. 'But what becomes of Mr. Harris?' asked a certain Miss X, a convert, albeit apprehensive. Nothing became of Mr. Harris. 'Lily Queen,' as the initiates quaintly put it, 'is inside of

Father, and consequently he of course stays in bed, and by getting into his arms we get into her arms.'

As we have said, Father was at this time a prophet of outstanding distinction, a sort of older edition of Mapah whose philosophy his strongly resembled. Like Mapah's his eyes were deep-set, glowing and mesmeric capable moreover of extraordinary modulations as was his deep-set, glowing and mesmeric voice. Whence he delivered himself, says Editor Strachey, of cryptic utterances and occasional impassioned letters, fascinating both men and women by their 'obscure force'. His most remarkable disciple, socialite, amateur adventurer, war-correspondent to *The Times* in the Crimea (both were Englishmen), suddenly forsook a life of adventure and social glamour in order to follow Father to the other side of America where he slept in a loft containing amongst other things empty orange boxes and was put to work cleaning out a cattle shed in solitary confinement under a vow of silence.

Solitary confinement for her too, when in 1868 his doting mother, Lady Oliphant, joined him under a similar vow of silence and an invitation to wash the handkerchiefs. Lighter work but a long apprenticeship, for when five years later Laurence, who had been given leave for a trip to England, brought back a bride to Brocton the couple found Lady Oliphant still washing the hankies. Father's mesmeric way. Before permission could be given to penetrate the inner mysteries of the cult apprentices were expected to work their passage by doing the chores under the equivalent of a prison sentence.

Unless, of course, like the Oliphant bride, a girl beautiful, refined and rich, they exhibited affinities with Lily Queen, in which case protocol permitted a less leisurely elevation.

And believe it or not Alice Oliphant, the bride, turned out to be as near as dammit Lily Queen's double, a coincidence Father lost no time in pointing out, together with its consequences, involving as it did an early visit through the only stairway to that star. Nonetheless it all seemed to work. For a time. In the end however, whether because Laurence Oliphant, the groom, who had been sent away by Father's divine command to a distant city brideless, found it inconvenient to be the husband of Father's counterpart, or because the death of his mother made him see things in a new light, trouble did break out. Whatever the reason, the prophet and his disciple clashed; hard words were exchanged; a law-suit was started to get the property of Laurence's bride out of Father's mesmeric hands – for into them it had got – and at last the bridegroom now distinctly angry retired to Palestine where he continued his unconventional career by purchasing the Plain of Armageddon and setting up a new establishment and faith based – and this is the interesting thing – on the pattern of the Brotherhood of the New Life. Believe it or not, despite his break with Father, Laurence still retained so passionate a belief in the cult of Lily Queen that with his own local improvements he set about teaching the theory of Counterparts to the population of the Holy Land, ably seconded by Alice, the bride, now likewise weevilled out of Father's mesmeric hands.

Alice as it turned out took up the running in a big way, leaping into bed with poor Arabs no matter how degraded or dirty they were – a thing she found, as she candidly said, 'a great trial' – in order to impart to them the Harris lore, re-styled Sympneumata. Quarrel though they might with Father they still, you see, passionately, dramatically, heroically, embraced his faith.

Aphrodite Without a Nightie

Of these eccentricities the popular view is the simple one, that while religious mania when it takes the other extreme of the scourge, the hair shirt or spiked-garters, can be treated with a certain facetious respect, those who use their religion as a cloak for secret doctrines, meaning licentious carnal rites, are fraudulent professors whose bad smell is not be disguised by the odour of unction they pump out like sanctified but ink-ejaculating squids.

Still, that view doesn't really hold water. Most of the devotees of practices like complex marriage and counterparts were labouring under strong religious compulsion; were in other ways temperate, industrious even saintly people; people we should call ideal citizens. Countless witnesses subscribe to the saintliness and sincerity of the great majority of these devotees, though Hannah Witall Smith, herself a famous evangelist who collected most of the examples given here, including the Oliphant story, thought them misdirected. Actually she never knew it but the Oliphants, those champion bed-getters-into, did later claim from deliberate religious conviction never to have consummated their own marriage. This she would perhaps have deplored along with their other practices; their sincerity she didn't doubt.

In another illuminating report she relates how at one of the Holiness Camp Meetings held through the warm American summers by the Methodists (who believe in sanctification by Faith) a few friends gathered one evening in a tent to wrestle with God under a strong compulsion to experience conscious Baptism

55

by the Holy Spirit. To which end 'their expectations and longings were wrought up to the highest pitch'. With good reason since at almost every meeting 'wonderful testimonies' were being quoted by those who had, as they believed, consciously received it.

Nonetheless on that particular night they knelt for two or three hours in the dark tent pouring out supplications and 'groanings that could not be uttered' without results for, alas, God wasn't playing. Why, no one could think; not anyway until one of the party, a girl, described later how the scales were peeled from her spritual eye to reveal the Holy Ghost 'in bodily form hovering in the air above the meeting, striving to come down into the heart of the people present. Try as he might, however, an invisible barrier seemed to hinder his approach 'any nearer than about four feet above our heads'. He pushed and pushed to get through, but the barrier seemed impregnable so that at last 'he was obliged reluctantly to give up the attempt'. The girl who saw the vision said in her heart 'O Lord what does this vision mean?' 'It means,' came the reply, 'that all hearts present are so full of themselves that it is impossible for me to find entrance, and it is of no use for the people to pray for the Lord to take possession of them unless they are first emptied of self.'

Of the sensual self that is; illuminating the curious way truth is interwoven with error in the philosophy of the physical thrill. Far from being disinterested or selfless these wrestlings are basically competitive, a sublimated form of D-sport comparable to the Try-Your-Strength machine at the Fair. To have a Revelation, to win a Conscious Baptism, to get a Divine Guidance even to bag a Remarkable Experience, gives you a lead if only by a short head over the other competitors. Great strength returns the Holy Ghost.

And being a physical game those who practise it start by using physical means. Shameful propinquity, the touch of bare flesh, might in certain circumstances be the right instrument to bring a Baptism or win a Revelation. Hence that quiet refined lady past middle age, evidently very intelligent, likewise a Christian mother highly esteemed by her fellow citizens, who confessed to Hannah Witall Smith 'there have been times that in order to help my friends to receive Baptism of the Holy Spirit I have felt distinctly led by the Lord to have them get into bed with me and be back-to-back without any nightgown between.'

She added, 'it has always brought them conscious Baptism'.

Soon, however, familiarity would make stronger measures necessary. The young Quakeress who in the same tent in the same story succeeded later in the evening in achieving a Baptism accompanied by symptoms of bliss and rapture suggestive of a physical climax became sold not long after on the idea that the Baptism was a physical every bit as much as a spiritual event. Hence the great aim of religious teachers should be to excite in themselves and others those physical thrills that accompany passion; manifest tokens, she had come to believe, of the union with Christ. In effect she became a witch and took to standing naked before her own teacher, who returned the compliment in the full frontal position, the point being that it was shame-making – i.e. physically exciting – to flout convention in so primitive not to say juvenile a way. This particular saintly sister ended by taking the Song of Solomon to be the exposition of the relation between the soul and Christ as the Bride and Bridegroom and 'confessed to me with great awe', says Hannah Witall Smith, 'that she really believed that Christ had come to her at night when in bed as the real Bridegroom and had actually had a Bridegroom's connections with her.'

Inevitable development of the religion of the physical thrill, the impulse of carnal surrender which has led other faiths and places to favour high jinks in the form of Temple prostitution, sexual rites, orgiastic revivals, blood-shedding, and other unsupernatural doings. Mechanical convulsions as well, induced by passing an electric current through the brains of converts eager to turn on. Wesley himself though for nervous disorders not conversions (as he anyway claimed) gave electric treatment to his flock.

5

THE TORMENTED CENTURY

The Crisis of Communism

Up to this point the whole argument has been in one sense a digression; indeed in view of the debt current English society owes to the seventeenth century, an irrelevance. Or would be were the debt acknowledged; in a society that looks no further back than the last round of pay restraints or further forward than the next round of wage demands, an action that seems rather remote. Hardly, one might think, the right climate for social engineering. Unless the situation signifies something more perhaps than the decay of an ethic or epoch – the passing of a system. None other in the view of this argument than the monopoly engineered by the D-kids (capitalism) upon the achievements of applied science. And insofar as one piece of engineering builds on the other the great, the insolent Baconian adventure by which OUT THERE, object of all his calculations, when observed with instruments sufficiently sophisticated, disappears in an electric charge; certainly no *thing*.

Anyone who can find purpose or meaning here should hang on to it since for most of us the secret is well kept. If the founding fathers of the sciences expected to reveal the purpose of their Maker in His Works or even his Methods or even his Person – as they did – they were to be disabused. After dismantling the world their grand analysis has made clear its total incapacity for any revelation beyond such matters as the superiority of bilateral to circular symmetry. Science in other words has disclosed its incapacity to interpret reality except in terms of its consequences in events or sense-data. In terms, that is, of our own five senses. Except to scientists hardly a surprising outcome; in a discipline coined to call the bluff of the metaphysicians what else would you expect.

Nonetheless, science, like parliamentary government and

personal independence and religious toleration and freedom of conscience, and private enterprise and democratic values and human rights – all products or beneficiaries of the puritan revolution – still provides the element in which modern Western society moves; as do some of its less orthodox hang-ups in the shape of the high jinks celebrated in the last chapter and widely enjoyed today. Their aficionados may not invoke the love of God but justify their actions to themselves by pro- or anti-antinomian devices straight out of the repertory of Christian liberty. In the light of which one can maintain that the shadow of Christian liberty still provides chiaroscuro in the twentieth-century scene; sometimes, thinking of Charles Manson et al, a sinister gloom.

What, oddly and ironically, we have lost, is the one thing all these notions were designed to foster, that picture of the good life which has teased the human mind since Adam delved and Eve span. Last put together in the century whose true heirs we of the twentieth are, the seventeenth; since then smogged out of memory by that later revelation, the industrial.

In consequence the plight of current man though he knows it not, is parlous and probably unprecedented. A horror comic wished on him by two centuries of greed and scepticism. The view that all was for the best in the best of all possible worlds lost credibility with *Candide* and the Lisbon earthquake; belief in free-will with the *Origin of Species*; faith in democracy with *Das Kapital*; man's humanity to man with *Mein Kampf*. As for the comforts of religion to most of us the Church no longer carries a decipherable message. One by one our faiths have been put out like candles round an altar after the priest has shut his book and stumped away. And with the extinction of each flame the once cosy prospect has grown greyer, then bleaker. Until now as darkness falls the outline of this vertebrate who in a sanguine moment when the ductless glands were working overtime had the presumption to christen himself *sapiens*, blurs. Blurs in a manner to suggest he's lost something more than a few hormones – confidence in the capacity to keep his own identity alive during this night of the soul; and with the loss thereof, momentum. A disc has slipped; the vertebrate threatens to become invertebrate.

Not only in degenerate Europe either. Something is slipping in the saucy optimism once a speciality of the New World. 'The more I have brooded upon the events which I have lived through myself,' wrote Walter Lippmann, 'the more astounding and significant does it seem that the decline of the power and influence and self-confidence of the Western democracies has been so steep and sudden. We have fallen far in a short span of time. However long the underlying erosion has been going on, we were still a great and powerful and flourishing community when the First World War began. What we have seen is not only decay – but something which can be called an historic catastrophe.'

This was in 1955, a year most innocent and optimistic democrats would regard as the high-water-mark of American power, influence, prosperity, prestige. Written moreover not because Walter Lippmann was a pessimist but because like others before and since he had terrifying presentiments. How could such a catastrophe be? About the fall of Rome the same question is still asked. The decline, you see, is not in terms of material assets or productivity or markets or know-how; in know-what, rather. Or know-why. And then only in regard to that Western world of the so-called democracies which has dominated events for the last two and a half thousand years. A sudden loss of confidence, shared not at all by other power blocs, amongst whom Asia is erupting, black Africa consolidating and the Communists coming on good. The prophets who proved decade after decade that the USSR couldn't take another five-year-plan were false prophets. Communism isn't cracking; it goes from strength to strength, both absolutely and relatively to its enemies, the democracies, who if not precisely cracking could be said to be disintegrating invisibly. They may not think they are, but the Kremlin thinks they are; it is this think which is postponing Armageddon. One doesn't waste energy bombarding the walls of a fortress whose foundations are sliding quietly downhill.

Such disorders may, hopefully, be less serious than our opponents believe, but one thing is sure; until we link up once again with our tradition the non-sequiturs of the twentieth century will never make sense, nor its chimaeras depart shrieking. In the few years since the end of the Second World War, while the British have lost an Empire, Russia has built a vast new one *in Europe*; of which she has mastered half. She has made a prickly satellite of China; she fosters revolution in Africa; she threatens the river of oil in the Near East and Iran, the jugular vein of our own industrial civilization. She menaces with dire menaces the rice bowl of Asia – Indo-China, Burma, Malaya. On the other side of the world in the Continental south she wages fierce political warfare with the aim of turning the US flank. Even in the Mediterranean which might be considered Anglo-American country Russia has the edge over the USA, as the American Admiral Zumwait discovered at the time of the Middle East war of 1973 when Moscow threatened to send an expeditionary force to rescue Egyptians unless America forced Israel to call it a day. Outnumbered by Russian warships by three to two and vulnerable to vast land-based air superiority the once august Sixth Fleet backed down in an act described by the *Daily Telegraph* as 'a direct, shattering but invaluable glimpse of a corner of reality'.

Some industrial inferiority the USSR may currently have, but with bombs and sputniks piled; with even greater natural resources; with seven times the man-power, a bloc, if you include those sovereign satellites now wooed or won by Moscow rising to a billion persons she is in a position to lead from strength because of her vast military potential and clear political purpose.

It sounds like arid intellectual theory. It worked. It worked in Russia. It is working today in China.

6

THE MANAGERIAL REVOLUTION

The Working Intelligentsia

Perhaps no single article of Communist practice has been more productive of misunderstanding than its double-think on the subject of the intelligentsia. The view of the Russian Revolution as a proletarian upsurge in which the bourgeoisie were given the brush-off in favour of horny-handed sons of toil waving hammers and sickles, fails to march at any point with the facts as they exist in the USSR, and, come to that, China. At the very centre of the Soviet system is a highly specialized bureaucracy and managerial class whose functions, while various, are quite specific at every level. Some are tribunes and administrators, others organizers and accountants, scientists and soldiers, technicians and engineers. Some are cheerleaders or pressure groupers scientifically trained to inspire, provoke, control, discipline and, finally, reduce to the rehearsed routines of gymnasium or parade ground the rude antics of the mob. A lot are cops.

Something quite other than the liberation of proletarian millions, almost the reverse, the preparation of an élite for their part in the control of the revolution and its serfs. In *Battle for the Mind*, a book which might be called 'The Intelligent Woman's Guide to the Mechanics of Indoctrination', William Sargent made a study of the shock techniques used by (and for) the cheerleaders in the excercise of their duties. His descriptions of brain washing and other conversion routines show to what lengths this applied science has gone in the Communist world. For the old-fashioned humanist it hardly makes agreeable reading. But it provides valuable documentation of the fact that the kernel of Leninism, regarded as a revolutionary theory, lies not amongst the long victimized urban or agrarian proletariat who are not much more than accessories before and after the act; it lies on the contrary with those who can perfect the machinery of control.

It is this, the mastery of the mechanics of control, that distinguishes Leninist from other revolutionary practice. Marxist theory did of course originally provide for a first stage in which the intelligentsia would guide the revolution in their capacity as a vanguard. A merely interim phase, however, in a sequence which would quickly resolve itself, leaving the effective dictatorship in the hands of the people proper. Which again was to be no more than a phase in the progress towards the classless society and the elimination of the State. If the sentimentalities implicit in this conception are clear enough today, so are the deceptions. How except by mass suggestion – or voting power – can a proletariat dictate? If such a question arose in Lenin's mind it didn't rattle one of the great realists of the age, who knew all too well that the future must and would look after itself. What mattered was the present and present control must be invested in the men who understand how a machine ticks, to which end he was careful to ensure that the revolutionary tune that set the heavy boots of the masses a-marching should speak even more beguilingly to the men who issued the commands.

His heirs have not reversed the policy. Whatever the West may think the vanguard is still the vanguard, pampered, petted, ogled, flattered. Nor is the appeal merely to self-interest. Deep motives of service are invoked in men and women in whom release therefrom has revealed the inefficiency and venality of the old order, notably the abuses connected with feudalism and laissez-faire.

The Managers

To a mind indoctrinated in conventional hammer-and-sickle rhodomontade concerning the liquidation of the bourgeoisie, the above may sound like a contradiction of all that Communism stands for in the popular view. It indisputably is. Facts when we look at them squarely tell the true story, the converse of the popular one, notably in the Middle East where although there is neither urban proletariat nor agrarian unrest and where as a consequence Leninism can't pose as a popular movement and might be expected to fall on stony not to say sandy soil the tide of Communism is running strong. No question here of the fascination, the 'peculiar fascination'* Soviet society exercises, or amongst what septs the charm is working: the managerial and

*Walter Z. Laquer.

professional classes. Why? Because these victims of feudal despotism aren't blind to the fact that a victory for Communism would put paid to the corruption and extortion that retard social progress, as well as to the feudal powers of the great Sheikdoms that perpetuate reaction.

Neither are they blind to the dramatic rise in status that would follow for themselves. Of such sanguine expectation it is customary in the West to say, 'Ah, poor fools, scorpions for whips', but this is seen by the people concerned as but another Western fiction, almost sour grapes. True, in 1928 the Comintern did once again reiterate that only in the first stage of the revolution would important parts of the party ranks be recruited from the revolutionary-inclined intelligentsia, and that implied that the dictatorship would eventually pass to the proletariat. But in practice – and this is something the revolutionary-inclined intelligentsia of the East, Near, Middle and Far, know well – nothing of the sort has happened. Despite the liquidation of sections of the bourgeoisie in the first days of the Revolution the managerial classes in close on half a century instead of modestly preparing their exit have been working like beavers to consolidate their victory. Have occupied all strategic positions, have dug themselves in, have demonstrated without much room for argument that in the home of the victorious proletariat, the Soviet Union, the managers have every intention of keeping the piano nobile for themselves. Far from losing ground they become every day a more privileged élite whose future perquisites are likely to increase rather than do the other thing, what time they move their families to the south to bask like sharks or wicked capitalists in the blue seduction of the Black Sea.

So one way and another the depressed professionals of the still feudal societies of the East are hardly to be blamed if they mutter amongst themselves, 'here but for the Grace of the Ancien Régime. . . .' Self-interest apart they see the Lenin line as the technique of modernization par excellence – is it their fault if modernization means the dominance of themselves, the managers? And is the Kremlin double-dyed when it whispers 'think, friends, where this will put you'? 'These men, the managers,' writes Eduard Heimann, 'are to be the masters, teachers, builders, makers of the new country and the new man: they will be lavishly equipped by Russia with all the facilities that can promote their work; rather than foreign bodies in their old communities, they will be the centre round which a new community crystallizes . . . there is no limit to the glory that is to come to them.' Put that way, whatever democratic freedom they would resign, as totalitarian specialists they would gain status and perquisites. Thus does the Party line appeal in one place to the urban proletariat, in another to the hungry peasantry, turning itself meanwhile where neither worker nor peasant have need of it and not vainly, into a movement of middle-class revolt against feudal reaction. Here lies the secret of the Revolution, the secret of its strength, of its power of continuity. It is not and never was even if it was meant to be a proletarian, it is a managerial, it is *the* Managerial Revolution. It is the revolution by which the technocrats have assumed the purple and mean to govern the world, an élite trained in the science of the conveyor belt whose job is to keep all the machines including the political one smoothly running. Running, however, according to a doctrine of technological rather than human relations, that is. Or of human relations only insofar as they can be dealt with by a psychology based on Pavlovian physiology. The more efficient the state machine, the more sophisticated the organization required to run it, the more firmly will the officers fasten themselves into the room on the frosted glass front of whose door is painted the magic word *Manager*. And the more essential will it be (to put the thing more justly) to give the initiative – together with the privileges and the perquisites – to those who daily demonstrate their organizational capacity.

Thus while the capitalist countries have been busy slapping down the managers in favour of those they manage in the pious belief that by doing so they were following at a decent distance the lead set by the Communist Party, the Party, by skilful diplomacy and careful propaganda, has been manoeuvring the managers (itself) into an impregnable position from which no man however massed will ever move it. Whether the Russians as a race are conscious of these trends is a question the outsider is not competent to answer; whether their rulers are, there isn't much question. Khrushchev's 1957 home-front tactics were explained (by Lilienthall) as a political manoeuvre designed to re-equate the Party with the managers (the bureaucracy and the army command) at a moment when there was some danger of the two falling asunder, with consequences less dangerous to the managers than to the Party because, should a split occur between it and the class that is the real power-holder, the Party would be in no position to enforce its authority. So much most democrats know. Yet as to what that knowledge means many care little and understand less.

Non-Military Penetration

Here lies the trouble. Of the two applicants for the post of 'Westernizer' or 'liberator' of the backward races and depressed peoples of the Third World one has a scientific method of proven worth ready to do two necessary things – release the revolutionary force of the peasant masses who would at the worst prefer to exchange a tyranny they do not know for one they know too well – then establish the managerial class as an élite privileged to manipulate this power. The other – democracy – has nothing to offer either except 'human rights' in quotes – nothing, that is, except platitudes (to which no one gives more than lip-service) about the quality of life and the equality of man and the sacred nature of self-determination and the charms of universal suffrage and the rightness of one-man-one-vote, and the dignity of parliamentary institutions.

Human rights, God help us. There you have the real predicament for the West, the one that makes the Russians rub their hands and feel they can afford to wait upon the efforts of their emissaries who span the globe with wolfish offers of help. Barring accidents the thing is in the bag. The routine de-imperialism of the ex-imperialist world, far from being a triumph for Western enlightened policy, only plays into Soviet hands, creating areas ripe for the Communist technique of loosening up those ready for the treatment.

For if the highly advanced political societies of Europe can't make democracy function smoothly, and they can't, how in the name of practical common-sense can you expect the primitive societies of Asia and Africa to do so? The Kremlin has no intention of leaving the backward and depressed in a state of nature. Let them toy with democracy, let their Colonial overlords force self-determination and majority rule and universal suffrage upon them; let democracy wreak its own ineffable destruction –no softening-up process devised by the most diabolical cloak-and-dagger men could more expertly prepare the unfortunate whom it will bring to confusion for the genuine if limited freedom it can ensure when self-determination, by breaking down the existing power blocs and spheres of influence, has left the way open for dictatorship, and so given the class within that society which must eventually take over – the working intelligentsia – a foretaste of independence and responsibility. A foretaste, that is, of the power which will be theirs when having mastered the role prepared for them they are ready to throw off disguise and get down to the real business of steering the corporate state.

Does anyone doubt that the policy of the Kremlin is to play the 'Free World' at its own game by using cliché democracy to incite backward races to claim their freedom and kick out their bosses, and so in the name of self-determination loosen the West's hold on the East? Whether democracy or dictatorship follows won't bother the USSR whose sole interest in the first phase of the operation is to excite the maximum number of nationalisms, and so in the name of emancipation effect the Balkanization of those parts of the world that were once in fee to the West.

After which the men in the Kremlin will need to do no more than sit back and await the moment when each new fledgling, shaken to its roots by war, intrigue, graft or tyranny, invokes the clean-up that will end in revolution.

However, one thing is certain. Since Korea and Vietnam went bad on the US the Kremlin's policies are based on the conviction that the West will crack or be cracked, and so let in an interregnum of anarchy or dictatorship, in which statecraft of the new corporate type will have an opportunity to provide the only alternative order to Western 'Protection'. In such a situation Marxism will collect satellites by the handful, with whose aid it can go on to dominate and indeed take over the UN and so identify internationalism with Communism. No fear after that of the UN not working.

Communism, then, has a message for every community at whose door it knocks, in particular the door marked *Manager*. It is one that is clear, consistent and beguiling. Nothing difficult here, no question of the advantages offered nor of the hard work demanded or the disciplines required. There is the revolution (throwing off the fetters), the entering into possession, the sharing of the labour and the fruits thereof, the discipline in the interest of the disciplined, higher living standards for the once expropriated arising from community of effort, the initiate neither dodging his own work nor expropriating his neighbour's, all being of equal consequence in the eyes of a paternal State which will let none starve even if it lets none opt out. Some, as we know, are more equal than others yet even these can be hailed as comrade by those who are less.

The psychology is simple but powerful, the story obvious but obviously sensible. Patently true, moreover, in the sense that its results in Russia and China have been electrifying. You don't have to be very clever to understand it or its implications.

Nor do you have to be a major statesman to see that those who do not, or do not want to accept it because they happen to be the other side will have to think up a better story. It won't have to be very clever or complicated. It might be even simpler, more obvious. It must, however, be believable.

When one looks at the other side (ours) one finds the unbelievable. We have no story.

Thug

THE CAPITALIST SOCIETY

To found a great empire with the sole
purpose of raising up a people of
customers may at first sight
appear a project fit only for a
nation of shopkeepers.
Adam Smith

7

SYSTEM BREAK

Crisis of Capitalism

Western man seems to have little idea how odd this thing of not having a story is. Well, yes, we had the American Dream but woke up. Earlier societies preened themselves on their life-style and set out to sell or impose it on their neighbours. Every kind of violence has surrounded the world-wide promotion of the brand image, secular or religious, not excepting the religion of love. All the West can settle for now is the concept of the sovereign individual, hailed by some good democrats as the best of all models for man and thus the best of all sales stories and thus the best of all reasons why the present argument is rubbish.

If only it were. If only the sovereign freedom of the individual were the ultimate end of the democratic machinery. Alas, democratic or not the machinery, being mere machinery, no virtue of any kind accrues to it until someone answers the burning question – *what* is a sovereign soul free *for*? Because if he doesn't know and won't be bothered to find out, his proprietary right in sovereignty or freedom becomes simply the institutionalization of purposelessness.

Free for what? That question the Communist doesn't have to answer because he can put the things the other way round. Free for anything you fancy, he says, so long as you carry out your social responsibilities. And the Party is careful to see your fancies conform to these responsibilities by telling you which freedom to fancy, then putting watchdogs on to make sure you fancy it. The Party is scared of freedom, hence the Gulag Archipelago. Democracy (foolishly) isn't scared. Only democracy enables the sovereign individual to ask the crucial question, free for what? And then goes on not to give a cuss whether the question gets an answer or not. Yet until it does get an answer that sovereign individual's sovereignty and so his freedom and so his democracy, and so his privacy and private initiative and private enterprise and private hot-line to Providence remain in abeyance, and so go by default and so are worth precisely nothing.

Do we anwer it, do we even ask it? We do not. Instead we speak of democracy as though it were a positive asset like a bank balance. It is the bank without the balance. The institution is there, doors open, ready to protect your investment but – in the absence of a balance to bank – it grows worse than frustrate, redundant. We talk of peace in the same way. Peace has no intrinsic value. Unless you know what to do with peace it hasn't even got a meaning. Which explains why peace is so much harder to handle than war, by comparison an open-and-shut job.

Acting out a similar deception the British operate as though the almost perpetual crisis of the economy springs from balance of payments problems or money supply or out-dated capital equipment, or because we don't improve our competitive position among exporting nations, or don't contain inflation, or don't fight unemployment, or don't accept the need for de-industrialization, or fail to offer consistent government policies, or, in the absence of restructuring, do nothing to buttress the perennially tottering £. Fantasies all, though real enough in their own context. In fact the situation is more desperate than explanations of that kind suggest. Behind specific fantasies there is a general fantasy. In a world that no longer shares a common set of values the only point on which all agree is that we don't know where we are going. None rises so high, said Cromwell to the outraged Cardinal de Retz, by which he meant that values are a better bet than a target. True enough in a general way but the situation is not quite the same in a society like ours where the values have sunk with the target so far beneath the wave, that no odds can be offered on either.

Still, on two pieces of news one good, one bad most people do largely agree. The good news is that technology can now dissipate poverty even in the Third World; the bad news, that amongst those who have already exchanged poverty for plenty the switch hasn't done much to bump up morale. The incidence of boredom, loneliness, frustration, violence, rootlessness, stress complaints, paranoia, drug addiction, alcoholism, suicide and murder – particularly among young people – had, by 1970, grown to such proportions that the Nobel Foundation organized a special conference to examine causes and possible cures for the world's malaise. Professor Arne Riselius's opening speech stressed the 'growing awareness amongst people of all nations that something is wrong with the world'. Here, as it always does, general agreement ended since the social engineers whose business it is to probe such problems, had, lacking a common perspective, no alternative than to invent personal ones founded on their own private opinions or absence thereof. The outcome? That hollow sound we, the unreformed, are all too familiar with when invited to change our life-style to complement the reformer's own. We never have. Never do. Never will; the only point of agreement between us.

For the British the real trouble lies as we have said before in the question itself which still remains ill-defined; the old story of not being able to choose between alternatives because it isn't clear between what alternatives one has to choose. The need, accordingly, is less how to seek the solution than how to define the problem; as to which there are several schools of thought ably developed in a chain of doom-watch best-sellers (*Rethink, The Collapse of Democracy, Astride the Two Cultures, Beyond the Energy Crisis, Crisis of Democracy, How to Avoid the Future, The Stagnant Society, Small is Beautiful, The Accidental Century, The Abstract Society,* etc., etc.) winding up for our purpose here with Alvin Toffler and *Future Shock*, a work that invites the reader to acclimatize himself to surprise in view of the paralysing effect on American presidents of the sheer number of futures available to a technology so sophisticated that it can make a monkey out of destiny by mass-producing alternatives at will. You pays your money and you takes your choice. Of destinies. Or Big Brother does.

But if it isn't in him or you to make a choice . . . what then? Anarchy? Dictatorship? Reds *in* not under the beds? Collapse of Western civilization as we know it?

Economic Man

Toffler is useful in pin-pointing a state of social confusion for which there's no cure– if cure it can be called – but his – if his it can be called. Namely, that in the absence of old-style destiny and the presence of new-style anomie, he argues, society must be prepared to undergo sudden changes – system breaks – a proposition all too easy to believe unless the answer given now suggests a less painful alternative. Based on a very simple logic, it can, as we suggest, be expected to clean up the mess in a surprisingly comprehensive way.

For though no one has troubled to use it or even recognize

its existence a key does incontestably exist designed to reveal not only what alternatives there are but which alternative to take, as the next section will, we hope, establish beyond all reasonable doubt to the satisfaction of those who do with good reason reasonably doubt it. Believe it or not this key will emancipate us from many, maybe all, false pressures or functional fantasies and do so by highlighting the causes of our frustrations in terms of the system break we are the current victims of. Decide, furthermore, the character of both the break and the system, the old system and the new; likewise the machinery required to take us out of one into the other. There is, you see, no crisis. Paradoxically, in view of all that we have said above and all of the many dire prophecies dreamed up in earlier chapters of this (not to mention others) book, *there is no crisis.*

No crisis? No more, anyway, than we have ourselves generated by deliberately misreading the omens. Anyone if he tries hard enough can create a crisis. Why bother to try though, when Providence, still our favourite schoolmistress, is dotting the i's and crossing the t's of that Baconian miracle with which she dotted and double-crossed Cromwell's. Because the same miracle can and will solve such real difficulties as there still are; create furthermore a climate in which that nasty piece of work, economic man, will for the first time in recorded history lose the initiative. Vanish, possibly for ever, or anyway walk for the foreseeable future in the shadow of his real master.

Oddly enough, however, that event demands another look at economic man's economy; to which end we propose in the next section to desert messianic day-dreams and other pious exercises in favour of the hard stuff of household management. Oikonomikos. The dismal science. For the sound reason that when things are as they are today, really bad, it often happens that the higher good has to be approached by way of the lower before the serious business can begin – 'You can't preach Christ to empty bellies' – and the West or our section of it is in that kind of plight. Not noticeably empty-bellied as it happens, but suffering a lacuna more difficult to find an antidote for – apathy. Or anomie. Empty hearted; the consequence of this crippling load of frustration. Which has left the British pretty well horizontal like their heavyweights. As of now the pressing need is to provide the bone-tired, the repressed, the frustrated, the bored, the disillusioned, the neurotic, the aimless, the disoriented, the angry, the violent, the flaked-out, freaked-out, bug-eyed and souped-up – a whole generation bled white of vital energy and adaptive intelligence – with a blueprint of a kind simple enough to show how they can defeat the conditions which are getting them and everyone else down. Or rather, how the march of events if properly encouraged will work that magic for them provided they show enough ordinary horse-sense not to obstruct the work of Providence by obdurately blocking the way. Forget North Sea oil. The only requirement now is a fresh look at our economic philosophy.

One qualification first, however. What follows is so simple, so obvious, so utterly without complication or guile that some sovereign souls may even suspect they are being mocked. Not so. To any addict of Baudelairean correspondences economics even of the most elementary sort occupies a key position in the eschatology of Salvation, as any disgusted reader may himself discover should he decide to read on.

8

MARXMANSHIP

Gamesmanship

If, with whatever reservations, the feeling spreads abroad that things aren't what they ought or used to be, it's fair to assume there's something, not necessarily rotten – wrong – in the State of Denmark. The question then becomes, is it the *state* of Denmark or the *State* of Denmark? Are the System or the People missing a trick, or, supposing one can be equated with the other, both?

Here is where Baudelaire with his Theory of Correspondences and mountains of hasheesh brings order into the discussion; for if thematic unity or essential concordance of any sort can be postulated of the arts, surely one must allow the same privilege to humanity and its institutions. Whence it follows, doesn't it, that a diagnosis of one will – *must* with any luck – reveal the nature of the other and so uncover whatever malfunction is operating, no one can say until it turns up in which.

More than this however. Unless hasheesh is already clouding our vision a chasm opens in the economic system itself when this method is applied. Revealing in its current efforts to function a conflict between principals who have no call to breathe the same air or occupy the same space. Though few will admit it in public the contradiction is total. Cross-purposes simply do not arise. Neither does reconciliation. Automation and full employment amount to a contradiction in terms, and one or the other must go. And here is where, by coming up against an opposition it was never groomed to deal with, our traditional economic philosophy disqualifies itself by its own limitations before the game begins.

One word of caution, however, before the game does begin. To achieve a fruitful result the subject of debate needs to be caught red-handed (like the electron) in the undisturbed state. Distinguishable, that is, from whatever another sportsman has made of it after upsetting the run of play. Games are a case in point. They indicate an impulse for play back there in the unconscious which pre-empts any cultivation of a particular sport. Yet it is open to question whether some games or anyway the way some people slaughter them, do not flout the sporting impulse and so distort the essential character of play.

The games people play with economics prompt this caveat since in every case one has to ask whether a given ploy flows from the nature of the game or from some arbitrary caprice of the player; he to be defined in the second case as a gamesman practising gamesmanship rather than an athlete discharging his debt to the laws of sport. The question arises in its most notorious form over the gymnastics of that testy genius who first played football with capitalism, flooring the opposition with savage elbow charges and jumping on the vital parts of any player who stayed down. Was he a prophet revealing the historic destiny of the economic process or a gamesman of the highest order practising gamesmanship of the lowest?

Since the purpose here is to follow his example in the economic field by analysing the composition of the institution itself, an obligation to enquire into his conclusions and the methods he used to come by them seems required. This involves something rather arrogant, a full frontal challenge to the father if not founder of historic process, whose achievement it was to harness the spleen of his ancestors to the mystique of his age and so, as he believed, forge the instrument of destiny that would realize a classless future for the Civil Society (his phrase).

The Dark Little Savage

To say he succeeded would be the understatement of the century. Today his faith has a congregation larger than Christ's. Remains the question, was his triumph the consequence of a correct prognosis or merely a spin-off of his own alarming will. About the will no question arises; about the man, a black bombshell erupting on the shop floor of the Victorian Age with a bang that could be heard across the whole Continent, many remain. Black because the bomb case was almost completely covered in hair – black hair, rooted according to the industrialist Nevissen in head, cheek, ears, nose, arms and hands. Safe, probably, to add shoulders, chest, belly, legs, though for confirmation his wife would need to go on the record. It was she who rechristened what went on under the hair as *my own dark little savage*, a signal of

affection, nay, devotion, never retracted even when his way of
life reduced her to nervous prostration, as it more or less
permanently did. And apt as well as devoted; for a savage he
was, short, rugged, truculent, intolerant, vindictive, gay, vain,
cynical, inhumane.

And black. After the hair the most startling feature was the
nose, by no possible stretch of the imagination Assyrian; on the
contrary snub. Chubby even, in eerie contrast to the eyes
described by the police spy who gatecrashed his home in 28 Dean
Street, Soho, as 'demonically sinister'. They (the eyes) reflected
his personal capital of disgust and genes; disgust at the greed and
venality of man; genes bequeathed him by another even
blacker bombshell, the fifteenth-century forbear, Jehuda Minz
a fierce and fiery Rabbi who before his death at the age of 10?
engaged together with Abraham, his even fiercer and fierier son,
in fierce and fiery feuds with any madman amongst flock or con
freres who dared to challenge either on the most minuscule
article of their faith. Their descendant, a Christian and a
Protestant but a man of his age and race, nauseated by cant of the
British kind, abominating the stupidity of poverty, resolute to see
history as an Hegelian process of law unencumbered by human
hocuspocus, radiated a similar fire; exercising (the police spy
again) 'an irresistible power on his surroundings'. Marx offers
a text-book example of the revolutionary *born*. Suckled by
Jacobins on the poisoned milk of the French Revolution, burning
thereafter to find the right kind of social demolition job, he
looked around, and lo, ideal material for any hit man, the crazy
disorderly house of capitalism, packed to the eaves with its
arrivistes, parvenus, profiteers, hoodlums, lackeys, pimps, bawds
– the hateful bourgeoisie, who had two-timed the Revolution and
brought it to naught.

First business, to startle the pimps out of their self-satisfaction
by blood-curdling threats of an awful end at the hands of their
victims, the proles. A simple matter thereafter to justify the
holocaust in terms of historic necessity (Marx's métier this – he
left the factual stuff to Engels); and let's admit it his success,
though he never tasted it, was enough to dominate the thought
and actions of the next century.

Here, however, one has to pause to ask whether his reading
of the omens was a valid one. Was he sportsman or gamesman?
The appeal to historic process is inadmissible because inconclusive;
as every publicist knows any pattern required by the Est- or
Disest-ablishment can be mocked up by a competent craftsman

weaving his tapestries of the past with one eye on their impact in the corridors of power and the other on his route to the bank. Some hold Shakespeare did exactly this for the Tudors; Marx's purpose was less servile and more honourable – to startle both rich and poor into revolutionary action – but his methods, intentional or not, were every bit as casuistic. The question thus remains, were they valid? Or on the contrary the brilliant ball-play of a grand master of conmanship.

Consider his own happy communist, classless, stateless paradise, lost nor ever yet regained, yet unregained regainable; the proletarian take-over of the means of production. The reader cannot but notice in his sneaky way how uncharacteristically Utopian (that word always had Marx reaching for his gun) this pristine idyll was. Yet how well adapted to his purpose always supposing that purpose was so far from Utopian as to be angled at a more mundane, more immediate, more practical and to a born iconoclast more entertaining end-product. None other than the disruption of the current Establishment and its brand-image, the middle class. In all the bourgeois beastliness of both.

The Bourgeoisie

That, anyway, was how it worked out, with, by evolutionary standards, lightning triumphs which still disguise – alas, declare it now we must – the magnitude of his transgression in double-think. Notice the shrewdness of the switch from social engineering to economics, the mystique of the day, a subject both trendy and ill-understood, not least by him; which explains along with Helene Demuth's bastard the years of toil in the Reading Room of the British Museum with at the last the birth of surplus value, that mighty mouse.

It paid off, however; the whole exercise brought him his enormous and enduring prestige amongst those he could neither punch-up nor patronize. Difficult here and hereafter not to feel that he saw himself as a sprig growing a bit higher on the social tree than Philansterie Fourier, commercial traveller, or Born, plebeian (his own word for the man), or Bauer, Mole, Cremer, Odger, Weitling, Lasalle, Harney, typesetter, shoemaker, watchmaker, carpenter, shoemaker, tailor, tailor's son, sailor's son. A wrathful Baron de Charlus of the Barricades maybe, truculent to his peers, partial to the peasants, reduced to nausea by the middle men – Marx was married to a German title and small vanities often play a part in inverse ratio to their importance.

Perhaps the need to placate this near-coroneted false self partially explains the refusal to earn a wage, likewise the cowardly behaviour towards a natural son begotten by him upon the sublime creature Helene Demuth, *bonne à tout faire*. Likewise his passionate determination to stay on top of the heap. Any rival who dared to make passes at the presidential chair always aroused the sleeping Jehuda Minz, not forgetting Abraham, his fierce and fiery son. 'I am,' he used to scream after imbibing enough hard liquor, those brilliant demonic black eyes (brown actually, but they looked black) snapping with malice and intelligence, 'going to annihilate him.' Café rodomontade, but symptomatic of the cerebral violence that underlay all his aversions. Mass production, for instance, a growing tyranny which even then was taking its toll. How unexpectedly we hardly realize today; nor how violently mainland Europe – craftsman, peasant, prince – reacted against it – against mechanization and meaninglessness, that is – Marx's alienation – the Germans with particular ferocity. One of the reactions responsible for the dolours of the twentieth century. 'We deplore Hitler but prefer Nazi-fication to Americanization,' was still the cry of German youth after the Second World War a hundred years later.

Of such crimes against the common human pattern he was not so much an observer as an exposer. The leading one in point of fact, burdened with the duty to crucify the perpetrators. These, he realized in a flash of enlightenment typical of his genius, must be hoist on their own petard, snared in their own snare, expropriated by their own expropriations, pounds, shillings, pence, bloodstream of the capitalist philosophy. Thereafter, to a master of polemic, seized like Baudelaire before him of the ineluctable inward relationship of all human activities one to the other, it was a simple step to work the trick already pulled on Hegel by standing the civil society on its head in order to bring the business others had left at the bottom to the top – the dismal science.

To which, on the grounds that survival depends on the processes of production, he proceeded in company with several other political economists to give pride of place and something more, control over the whole social scene. Fair enough; *Chaque à son goùt*; after all Saint Simon had been there first; nothing here to get hot under the collar about – not anyway until the suspicion dawns that something else besides Hegel and the civil society has been stood on its head.

Yes indeed. The argument itself. Inviting the evil suspicion that cause and effect have been transposed: by a conjuror whose trick consists in working backwards from an already determined end to the symptom that might be plausibly advanced as its cause; in this case the expropriators he had set himself to stalk, corner and bring down well before the reason or means for their extermination was vouchsafed to him. To which end the transference of the debate from the political to the trendy and little understood economic field where few would question the train of thought because few would understand it, should make it easy to startle the living daylights out of his adversaries without incurring real resistance from any but the clever fellow-travellers he was well equipped to gun down.

And that was what it was – easy. And oddly enough in view of the disingenuity of the exercise some of the conclusions rang true even when their premises were false. Until the last round-up, that is, when what was artificial in the case did in the end make nonsense of his basic weapon, the dialectic.

And worse, obscure the real nature of the revolution taking place in front of those demonic eyes. In this really extraordinary almost inimitable piece of situation comedy hindsight allows us to surprise the guru of historic process with his trousers down; so dazzled by that twopence-coloured fantasy of expropriated expropriators dangling from every lamp post that the reality in front of his eyes – the Distributive Revolution – or Revelation – dismissed by him as dirty commerce – left him merely grinding his teeth. As he was determined to see it, a blackleg phase in productive relations whose perpetrators, the moneyed mobsters and their molls, would pay a heavy price in blood and tears.

Thus did the great revolutionary disdain, misrepresent, reject – indeed abandon – the greatest revolution bar none in economic history, the penny-plain but genuine and totally archetypal convulsion he was the angry spectator and should have been and in some sense was the unwilling prophet of.

9

THE THEORY OF CONTACTS

Loss-of-confidence Trick

Having accused Marx of worse than error – guile – the argument must now make good its accusations against him or retire in disorder. The second course though tempting would be discreditable, granted, yet in view of the Master's tremendous achievement in double-think the first can hardly be embarked on without trepidation. The only way to reduce the exercise to manageable proportions is to cut out all the in-fighting and return to first principles – first principles in the shape of the dialectical pattern of the science, established before Marx appeared on the scene. A sensible course because this provides evidence of a kind that unless blinded by bile, boils, ambition, hubris or double-think, a rational mind ought to be glad to accept without further question. And so dispense with the kind of 'critique' he enjoyed making of the infamous errors of Saint Simon, Lasalle, Prudhon and a long line of (to the Baron de Charlus) creeps, casuists or crawling nonentities. For the simplest possible reason. The basic formula that carried his, the Baron's, own argument through countless pages of turgid rhetoric, namely the equation of power – all power, economic, sociological, political, moral – with the relations of production was a school-boy howler of the first order. Had he, Marx, bothered to look at the social scene with the eye of the prophet he professed to be, rather than with the rage of the inconoclast he really was, his own masterful intelligence would have shown him that in a world where the industrial revolution had achieved a break-through for an alternative bunch of activists production was no longer in command of its relations.

For this error there is every excuse. With unimportant exceptions human politics stretching back into the mists of the Flintstone era have been involved with scarcity, and scarcity in whatever form involves one way or another a production economy - an Establishment dependent, that is, on its productive potential. *Dependent*, because right up to the twentieth century it was touch and go whether there would ever be enough goods to go round. Scarcity is the dynamic of a production economy, too many people chasing too few goods, with the prizes going to the fastest workers, in both meanings of the word. Production – that is scarcity – economies of one sort or another have existed (with minor exceptions like the Phoenicians or Venetians or the Bedouin of the Hadramaut) throughout the habitable globe from the time settlement first took place right up to the nineteenth century. The correlated political set-up can thus be described legitimately in terms of class since scarcity, which gives a production-economy the initiative, involves a Darwinian struggle for survival in which the weaker brethren gravitate to the bottom, and the stronger to the top of a social pyramid built on ownership of the means of production, or, more accurately, control of the means of consumption. Inevitable consequence, class divisions, as inequalities gravitate by electrolysis like to like; and by the same token evoke those paternalistic or feudal dictatorships which still rule the Third World. Though even there the grasp weakens. Capitulating not without a struggle to another as novel as familiar – machinofacture (Marx's word), structured by a new élite, the hateful bourgeoisie, obsessed with mass production. *Mass* production. Demanding more than the *power* of production, the *force* of *promotion*, by Marx dismissed as that abject activity, commerce. Had he admitted the authenticity of this revolution which he and Engels described with unmatchable invective in the first half of the *Communist Manifesto* and then in the pursuit of their obsession misinterpreted as wicked capitalism and all that saliva, Marx might have used his commanding genius to rationalize a movement which by raising living standards was (much against its will) steadily wiping out the proletarian world as the necessary means of satisfying the machines and their machinofactured lust for markets.

Marx observed the trend, needless to say, and even admitted its necessity, yet was denied the agony of applauding this near miraculous development by his own urge to crucify the genii thereof. Instead, visibly boiling, he performed a literary gymnastic almost as marvellous by representing the miracle as a wicked act of exploitation that must end in violence between the haves and the have-nots. A confrontation or class struggle which could only happen, if at all, under a production economy of the sort that was rapidly becoming a dead duck. Followed by the dictatorship of a proletariat already in his own lifetime breaking ranks and vanishing into suburbia. The last thing he meant to make was an honest appreciation but the effort, had he made it, would have raised him to grand master of a new dispensation and the architect of that destined to follow; which may well have some of the features of his own Utopia.

The distortions were flagrant, but it isn't difficult to see why an evangelist wedded to the idea of violence perpetrated them. So long as one thinks in terms of the ownership of the means of production alone the dialectical conflict can be found within the ranks of the producers – the expropriators – and their victims – and used as a pretext for a declaration of war (and war was what Marx was at all costs determined to declare). Nonetheless, in the one man who had brought economics and dialectics to bed in official wedlock his perversity in shrugging off the union he had engineered was a disingenuous ploy which destroyed the validity of his case and took him grinning venomously way off course to an already predetermined off-course destination: the shooting war. Once there everything else fell into place. So long as the debate could be confined to the battle for production he was sitting pretty because a shooting war was still a reasonable presumption.

But what right has a student of dialectic to confine the debate to one principle, the productive, when there are others with an equal claim to be heard? For a fuller understanding of the Marxian aberration it is only necessary to remind oneself once again that on the economic front, unlike the historic, a genuine dialectic exists whose operation gives us an insight into matters of great moment including the structure of society itself.

Conmanship

Why then did Marx the founder of dialectical method turn his back on majestic generalizations which provide the science with a simple yet sublime dialectical structure? Let the reader ask himself this question. One explanation only fits the bill: in a genuine dialectic no conflict is involved – no more anyway than the next few pages reveal which is no real conflict at all; yet conflict – blood and thunder – nature red in tooth and claw – was essential to his nature as to his case. His parody of the economic situation of his day had no other purpose than to clobber his victims; and it did. A brilliant but malignant exercise which has sown incalculable disruption owing to the almost unbelievable imbecility of its dupes. Economic history is not, as Marx maintained, the history of the 'relations of production' – economic history is the relations of *production* versus the relations of *consumption* versus the relations of *distribution*: the reciprocal give and take between three powers each not only sovereign in its own right, but using cultural, political and economic methods antithetic but complementary and compatible with its opposite numbers. To safeguard the rights of each and to control their interplay, their product, the State, legislates, then administers the rules. So long as three contenders are around a referee there must be without whose kindly intervention the tensions inseparable from their intercourse might get out of hand. The classless society, yes; the Stateless society, no.

Production

Obvious as it is, this, the true dialectical situation Marx made use of only when he had to, and in pursuit of his obsession was careful to misapply. Consequently he never bothered with the ultimate questions regarding supply and demand, whether they signify something more relevant to the human condition than their economic role implies. Do they correspond to some more transcendental reality; some principle within the social body significantly more meaningful than appears on the surface? Are they what Baudelaire would have called symbols or allegories? Do they for instance represent within a society, state or person a nature that is itself tripartite? *Production.* When we say we *produce* what do we really mean? Does the notion *correspond* to any drive in the body social that could be treated as a control?

Production. The ability to produce. A creative process? In a manner of speaking, yes – unless one chooses to stand strictly on etiquette and maintain that true creation can only be *ex nihilo*. In which case economic man can be said to create only at second hand: procreator. For an earthling the basic stuff of creation comes from a star, the sun, which bombards the surface of the earth with energy; but in a form the earthling can make only partial use of until such time as the energy so released turns itself into water, vegetation, coal, oil, fur, flesh. Then, unless it can be taken neat, he taps or cuts the stuff up, modifies and processes it, so diverting the energy to his own use. No real difference whether he paints a picture or cultivates the soil, the procedure is the same – the energy already in the soil, or within that product of the soil – himself – is diverted into forms capable of being eaten or used by Man.

Diverted, you observe, meaning modified, changed, processed, man-handled, manufactured. Making means changing. The essential act in this operation? *Differentiative*. Taking energy *undifferentiated* or not usefully *differentiated* and making it by *differentiative* treatment humanly available. Hence the producer: a character whose business it is to put energy through a course of *differentiation* and to go on doing so until it assumes a form he can use. The more various the *differentiations* the better. We label them all collectively 'production'; press always for more or more varied, or, as it is called, 'higher' production.

Consumption

So far so good. But what's it all for, this perpetual diverting of energy from sun heat, coal, fur, oil, sand, grapes, water, grass, milk, flesh, into steel, automobiles, leather jackets, plastics, cuts off the loaf? This man-handling? What does he, the earthling, do with all these things? The answer is even more of a platitude than the question. He *produces* in order to *consume*.

Do not gnash the teeth, dear reader. This commonplace is one of outstanding genius. Whoever first thought that sequence up had nothing to learn from Lao Tse. We produce in order to consume. Why do we consume? We consume in order to perpetuate an identity. The producer act is not an isolated piece of business, a private exercise; it is on the contrary one term of a reciprocal movement. And here, at the very throat of the producer we have the teeth of the consumer, the man who in whatever useful form it comes, grabs energy for his own purpose. The purpose! To turn it into himself. The producer busies himself differentiating energy; the consumer neglects no opportunity of reducing it in whatever variety to one identity, his own. Including of course the various personal extensions that turn an environment into a habitat. The producer differentiates energy, the consumer unifies – identifies – it. The greater the variety of goods (the greater, that is, the differentiation of energy) the higher a society rises in its own self-esteem. But always such variety is being employed to one end, *the persistence of that society*. Energy in a huge variety of forms is being differentiated to create and keep in being a persisting identity. The producer is giving energy many identities, the consumer reducing energy to one identity.

Faced thus with a tension between two ways of life, productive and consumptive, we are justified as planners in asking how that contradiction is to be resolved, and since we know the answer

– distribution – happy to give it. Not so happy about the word, though, which fails to assert one all-important qualification; that the movements of goods and services involve also the movements of those who supply them; and these are in turn determined by the *distribution* upon the land surface of those who produce and consume the services and goods supplied. Another way of saying that the distributive network embodies not only the milkman's rounds but the cow and the milk and the people who drink it: *the pattern of settlement itself.*

Which came first, the pattern of services or the pattern of settlement, is a hen-egg type of question of no consequence at all. As patterns they are interchangeable since each is conditional upon – indeed the product of – the other. So much so that variation in either will involve corresponding changes in both. Society is, in the simplest sense, its distributive pattern, and that pattern embodies all relations developed between producer and consumer. A case, this, in which the medium *is* so irrefragably *the message* as to entitle one to say society *is* its contacts.

Or communications. Lacking which relationships, no society can come into existence, since the boundaries of a society are the limits of its communications, i.e. contacts, i.e. distributive pattern. A contraction in communications will entail an equivalent contraction, dislocation of communications an equivalent dislocation, growth of communications an equivalent growth in the society under observation.

And in this word 'communications' must be included every possible contact, act of transport, means of combination; every speech, jest, cable, film, letter, painting, road, car, train, ship, pavement, drain, larder, house plan, hedge, gun; every form of communication from those good ones that keep armies fed in the field to those evil ones that corrupt good manners – all forms of contact, all relationships, from the lover's to the salesman's, from the bomb to the British telephone system, boasting at the time of writing contacts to the tune of some 3,000 million.

We are now in a position to cram all our clichés together into one sentence by saying that amongst a multitude of conforming dissenters (or dissenting conformers) the interplay of productive and consumptive movements by demanding a distributive pattern evokes the organization we call a society. That distributive pattern is a pattern of contacts *and nothing else*. That pattern of contacts *is* the society. A civilization is, speaking in economic and sociological terms, a society that has achieved an intricate pattern of contacts.

Obvious? Naturally. The next chapter sets out to apply the obvious to human nature, an even more perilous adventure, one, nonetheless, that has to be attempted if Hoffmann's nasturtiums are to be allowed the freedom of their siren smell. The trouble bubbles up from the same source, for unlike Galbraith's conventional wisdom (the wisdom which sounds good but isn't), the received wisdom which once sounded good and was, grows from perpetual use over the years so battered that the educated guesser tends in mere self-defence to leave it out of his calculations lest he be convicted of cliché. An unlucky event for the present debate, dealing as it is forced to do with the banalities, almost the bromides, of everyday conversation; in this case the three tremendous truisms on which the science of economics rests called by Malthus the first, greatest and most universal principles of political economy.

Clichés nonetheless. The price paid for genius, by Baudelaire defined as the ability to dream up a new commonplace. In this case three. Self-evident the instant they were coined, thenceforward good for all time, creating within events however intricate or sophisticated a huge simplification to which all contacts bow. Before that semantic deadline social relationships were economically meaningless or anyway unstructured; after – every action on earth had an anatomy.

THE GAMES PEOPLE PLAY

Adeste Fideles

At the time we are speaking of the technological dilemma was so new, so radical, so utterly without precedent, so intrinsically unique, so outrageously emancipatory, that any seer, even Marx maybe, should be forgiven for making a travesty of the omens. Jan Romein, the Dutch historian, dramatized the situation in his invention of CHP and the CHP man. Throughout history the way of life of the normal human being wherever his pad, India, Asia, Africa, the Americas – medieval Europe even – the Third World today – justified he felt the assumption that Western technocracy is an aberration of and act of alienation from what can be called the common human pattern or CHP and he who still conforms to it, the CHP man. The contradiction is there in sufficient strength to make Romein's point even while the Arabs are buying up Europe. But his case rests surely less on a common human than on a common economic pattern. One moreover numbered as to its days, a life-style that will grow progressively more un-common as the production economy that has stamped its signature on history for centuries, indeed millennia, goes out of business. Strip the CHP of its CH and you are left with a P, a P for pattern, a P for production, a P for *production pattern* – a pattern – and this is the point – totally idiosyncratic; unique to the *production leit motif* in its aboriginal form. Wedded, that is, to the concept of scarcity, the ark of the covenant of old-style production morality. Peculiar, too, to the mores of what can properly be called a production economy. Strip the CHP man of his CH and he becomes what he really always was, a P-man, no more, the victim – or beneficiary – of all the pros and cons of that almost P-for-paleolithic producer's ethic now in retreat from the D-offensive.

For his deceit in declining to take the next, the crucial, the significant one, the step into a dialectic of economics, omitting which the whole exercise becomes meaningless, Marx must take the responsibility. For if there's a P-for-production economy there will also be a C-for-consumption economy and a D-for-distribution economy. If relations of production, then relations of consumption, relations of distribution. Antithetic relations in each case administered by different types of people: producers, consumers, distributors, or (in the interest of a later argument), P-cocks, C-chicks, D-kids. Types rather than classes, horizontal rather than vertical divisions. Not sequential either – one behind or under the other, busting or ousting it after the pattern of class as presented in the Karlist Opus – or Oeuvre – on the contrary co-existing, each doing its own thing with interesting repercussions on its neighbours. Seeing that it was he who elected himself as dialectician extraordinary to the civil society and remembering that much of what he said was on target, how strange, how very strange, that in acknowledging one principle only, the productive (and demoting the others to mere hangers on) he, Marx, from spleen and Jehuda Minzidry, managed to by-pass the three vital statistics laid out right there on the economic table for all to see in favour of an exposé of the class war, still operative, true, yet restricted to a production economy whose days were numbered. Palpably warped, the whole exercise, pre-occupied as it was with abuses already overtaken by events or just about to be, as the atmosphere of built-in obsolescence indicates. In one department, moreover, a plain miscarriage of justice; misdirection of the jury rather. When the first-ever take-over by a D-for-distribution economy is smeared as dirty capitalism things have sunk pretty low. To the gutter in fact. Though some of the fringe benefits may have been both dirty and capitalist to discuss the whole revolution in such terms was inexcusable. In consequence this stupendous event went not only unhonoured, distorted; not only distorted, dishonoured; what time the rigid reign of the dark little savage discouraged lesser prophets from establishing other explanations for the phenomenon than exploitation or expropriation. Distortion and misrepresentation on this scale has clobbered any claim the master staked for a dialectical approach to the history of the science, since under his presidency of the Court, the evidence for the defence was disallowed in toto.

Why? Since none but an imbecile would suggest that Marx failed to understand the niceties of supply and demand, the only possible explanation of his tactic comes back to ancestor worship. Jehuda's, needless to say, fanner of feuds, for whom the crimes of new-style capitalism must be represented as another act of skulduggery by those rapscallions, the expropriators. Hence the focus on production. Hence the relegation of P's other buddies, consumption and distribution, to the inferior status of 'relations' – poor relations – the poor relations of production. That gave him and Minz a clear field of fire against such dark Mancurian mis-deeds as were sent down south for target practice by Engels when Engels himself was not galloping after foxes with that bulwark of Blimps the Cheshire Hunt.*

The Distribution Economy

Without any greater demand on expertise than is required by familiarity with the words production, consumption and distribution, let us now consider the true situation in the light of what the science itself reveals. The first principle to be clear about is the one Marx was determined to misrepresent, the fact, obvious enough to any normal brain, that while antithetic all three principles are complementary. They prop each other up. No chance of a shooting war even when argument between the partners grows warm. So to get his shoot-up Marx had to go back two centuries to the Cromwellians and disguise the puritan revolution as dirty capitalism. Or dirty commerce. Because as activists they burned to apply science to productive social purposes the puritans could be smeared as crooked operators exploiting the sons of toil by snide exercises in trade. One of his dirtiest words, 'commerce', used anywhere, anytime in the cause of guiding expropriators towards the tumbril.

The casuistry is clear enough. Yet exploitation and other similar heavily charged words have so intoxicated the air we breathe that our vocabulary has drunkenly accepted them as self-evident truths. If for the duration of this debate their existence can be ignored a different picture will emerge. Of an economic infrastructure that when challenged exposes, as Marx neglected to do, more than the economic – the human – the common human – pattern, rather different in character, admittedly, to Jan Romein's. One, nonetheless, that on the Baudelairean principle reveals society as itself tripartite, vulnerable to three counterbalancing pressures not unlike – if we may backtrack to the games people play – those at work in

*For this dissident activity Engels's excuse (humorous possibly) was that, come the Revolution, horsemanship learnt in the hard school of the Cheshire Hunt would give him credibility as a European cavalry leader.

Rugby Football (Union or League) where opposing teams of forwards, each on the face of it shoving against the other, create in that superficially hostile act an equilibrium, the scrummage – society itself – whose persistence depends on the capacity of each team to apply its weight where the other can engage it. Reciprocal action between opponents whose survival as scrummagers is dependent on the resistance of the adversary – society. Society, like the scrum, would collapse were either side to bite the dust or, come to that, over-react fist or bootwise in what would then have to be called war.

This is not war. Here the difference between conflict (war) and sport (reciprocity) sticks out a mile. In war the greater 'power' aims to *consume*, i.e. ingurgitate or take over the lesser, whereas the scrummage as an organization depends on both sides remaining equal and opposite. Intact. Moving up or down field if you like in the direction dictated by the burlier bottoms (or crabwise, three dimensions being native to this triangular rugby) yet never risking a push-over that would collapse the scrum. A curious sport in which nothing remotely like a goalpost is provided by the management since in common with the Caucus Race or Eton Wall Game no one ever wins, except, as in rugby proper, the man with the whistle, the referee (or State). Whose job it is to see that the tensions set up are kept up, that none is too small or too great; that that team which shows its fitness on the day gets the edge on the others and so the ball. Without denying that tempers sometimes flare and fists fly the fact remains that this resort to arms is essentially reciprocal. To remain intact the scrummage requires counterbalance between friendly rivals.

Consider now the awful consequences that would follow were some sorcerer by evil sortilege or gramarye to translate this platonic contest from the playing- to the battle-field, serving one side alone with secret instructions to wage war to the death. Except for the secrecy this was exactly what Marx did and preened himself on doing. With marvellous intuition he perceived the essence of the situation, even to the need of allowing 'commerce' to complete its mission amongst the weavers of Manchester, or, come to that, India; then, true to the tradition of ancestor Minz, perpetrator of feuds, he rejected with ferocity the reciprocal ideal in favour of Hegel's concept of conflict; and by substituting antipathy for antithesis succeeded in arranging a shoot-out between the teams which could only end in the collapse of the scrummage. Of Society itself, that is.

Total disaster, the fruit of a deliberate mistake, and one of which we are still the victims in so far as most people on either side of the Iron Curtain see communism and capitalism as on a collision course, lethal to one or the other, or, in view of the bomb, both. Not a pretty picture but one that is in our power to re-vamp merely by stepping rather quickly back from the jungle to the playing field. There, while still, let's face it, a bit of a scrummage the practical business of playing a part in the economic and also the political game offers each player a bit of sport, a choice of three teams, a chance to apply his abilities fruitfully in the frame his temperament responds to, and protection from abuse under the rules of the game as well as a lemon to suck at half-time. Absolutely nothing here to win except the initiative. Heads in hock, arms interlocked, torsos kept off the floor only by courtesy of their rivals' counter-offensive, they play this endless game of scrummanship, each team dependent on its adversary for survival.

Initiative, you observe. Though a game no one ever wins the medals go to the side gaining the initiative and so the ball, or since rugby is the game we write of, that ovoid thing – the egg – the golden egg.

Though for centuries the producers had been having it all their own way, with mass production a change came over the game as the initiative began to pass slowly but surely to the toughies of the distributive arts; who now found it unexpectedly easy to shove the others downfield. And finally – although it did not happen until our own time – this distributive arm (what Marx called commerce) gained the ascendancy. Today, in the West, we have a *Distribution Economy*, meaning a set-up in which producer and consumer find their policy *dictated* by the team who promote and market their products. An epoch-making development indeed, unattempted on the grand scale since through no fault of their own the Romans tried and failed. Today it has been realized: on the strength of a new distributive ploy, mass production, which we must now discuss, involving that newly enfranchised race of activists, the D-for-distributive kids, with their lust for sales campaigns, publicity, promotion, propaganda, private enterprise, markets, money, contacts, communications, networks.

MASS PRODUCTION

Potato

In view of the above it may appear obvious that the D-kid has no
genuine place in the production team or strategy and thus no
foothold on the shop floor; still less a seat in the boardroom,
since except by broadcasting its products his claim to turn the
wheels of industry is nil. After all *making* things (manufacture) is
loosely definable as a producer operation so one might expect the
theory as presented here to maintain that the bias in all
production is P. It isn't quite as simple as that. Take for example
the basic food of the twentieth century (potato crisps, one
assumes). Here it becomes clear as the action progresses that the
productive act of potato growing – 8,000 acres somewhere in
Lincolnshire – can and for economic purposes must be distinguished from the *distributive act* of marketing millions of little
flat things with an air bubble in the middle. One crisp,
produced unmassed, might pass for a producer operation throughout, from the planting of one potato to the implanting of one
air bubble; so might a few more. When to satisfy the *demand*
8,000 acres of fertile East Anglian mud have to be dedicated to
the raising of little flat things with an air bubble we begin to
have doubts. Production is involved in a big way it goes without
saying, but it also goes without saying that we are in the presence
of a double act in which the process of manufacture, though
anterior to is provisional upon a promotional programme. There
is an act of production and an act of promotion and in this
case the act of promotion – beguiling billions of crisps into
millions of stomachs – has the priority and holds the initiative
even though production and consumption are still involved. In
fact the distributive impulse dominates – almost monopolizes –
the project, at the managerial as well, as, alas, at the operational
level; machine hands who might once have had a potato-raising

brief now tend to become mere crisp duplicators, exercised over but one process in the operation, the bubble. Or perhaps not exercised at all, a notorious tendency in the practice of mass production which leads one to conclude that in view of its declared purpose – the widest possible propagation of bubbles – the production thereof is less the second term of a P-equation than the first of a D-. Meaning in a sentence that the conveyor-belt is a distributive gimmick and mass production a D- dodge.

Perhaps one may be allowed to say that again. Production and mass production do not come out of the same stable; indeed have nothing whatever in common. Awful errors have been committed in ignorance of this fact. Mass production is the mark – almost the trademark – of a distribution economy and needs to be identified with all the other monkey tricks practised by the marketing fraternity in their rage to kick goods and services around. The distinction is important – vital indeed – because when more than one economic life-style is available the machinery a society decides to use determines what particular economy has gained the initiative.

Capitalism

Anyone who accepts this summary will agree that a serious analysis would establish the existence of three types of economy sponsoring three types of work executed by three recognizable types of people of whom the third can be distinguished as responsible for capitalism in its current Mogulesque form; the D-for-distributive arm. Developing whether for good or ill its own specific economy, as a distributive offensive under the forcing tactic of mass production. The same pressures invoke vast marketing operations which span the globe in the form of multi-million multi-national multi-product conglomerates, buttressed by a vast army of D-types, importer, exporter, broker, wholesaler, retailer, entrepreneur, contact man, investor, speculator, company promoter, rep, canvasser, commission agent, advertising agent, travel agent, commercial traveller, PRO, publicist, publisher, journalist, tout, huckster, barrow boy, spiv, profiteer, racketeer, black marketeer – a cross-section through the great host who make it their business to sell mass production to the world. Creating consumers, that is.

Not that under this revolution production lost urgency; it merely lost face. The speed of the D-offensive carried all before it achieving a miraculous transformation from common human pattern to cybernetic man. Who thereupon grabbed from the P-arm the scrummage's initiative and started to raise his own kind of merry hell or as much as his playmates would buy. Some were not amused and accused the D-initiative of anarchy, yet not much difference of opinion can exist as to what the D-offensive has achieved: the greatest economic bonanza bar none in human history. Failing which, most of its critics would still be toiling in the sticks to keep their cadaverous loved ones in beet and other nutritious roots; provided always plague, tuberculosis, the pox, the bloody flux (dysentery), King Cholera, child mortality, the rope or Botany Bay had not already cured their bacon. And if in the pre-D-kid economy you happened to find yourself by a throw of the dice Botany Bay bound your prospects would be those of the second fleet of three convict ships whose arrival (at Port Jackson, Australia) revealed when the hatches were removed a 'ghastly company of sick or dying' – 486 out of a full complement of 1,017 souls. Of these 267 were already under the waves, 'slung over the ships' side in the same manner as they would sling a cask'. Of the 250 or so who could still put one foot in front of another, most were so weak they 'could hardly attend themselves'.

In happy contrast to this unpolished way of dropping in the drop-outs wicked capitalism's provision for the human equivalent today has Port Jackson,* not weeks or months but hours distant, serviced by Jumbos that make two stops only on the way. Well equipped furthermore with every convenience the civil society can bestow including rounds of beef, golf, martinis, social calls and lamb. So much even Marx admitted, muttering into his beard, since in the gentle art of spreading wealth around no system has ever had remotely comparable results.

Too many results indeed. Too much success. Success is in danger of becoming the Nemesis of capitalism.

*Sydney.

TYPES OF MEN AND WOMEN

A Dialectic of Types

As a science sociology began more or less with the attempt to classify types of men, yet, curiously, few since Le Play and Comte has seriously persevered with the idea. The assumption seems to be either that people are identical which we know to be untrue, or differ so much that no useful purpose is served in trying to typecast them.

Yet this view is flatly contradicted by their behaviour in ordinary life. Social intercourse and business enterprise involve much typing of others, whether productive or not is hardly the point; the itch is inherent in human nature even if no classification has so far turned out to be fruitful. Le Play's own formula, for instance, by Geddes improved into place-work-folk. His claim for the Valley Section that out of the place arises the kind of work and out of the kind of work the kind of worker made hardly any headway. And hardly any sense. Even if some perpetual peasant does lurk behind the pearl tie-pin of the banker the fact, if it is one, hardly throws light on either banking or the peasantry. One can't say the same, naturally, of Jung's intraverts and extraverts or W. M. Sheldon's endomorphs, mesomorphs and ectomorphs or Eysenck's function types or the shrinks in general, yet the difficulty of sorting out a common factor derived either from statistical procedures or theoretical postulates or body types based on hormonal activities remains. Despite the reproaches hurled at Le Play above, classification by type of work still seems a reasonably pragmatic approach.

There is, of course, the risk that because so many people work in occupations uncongenial to them typing them in this way is misleading. It might be more useful to look at the matter the other way round. Do occupations themselves differ sufficiently in kind to draw out specific capacities in the worker, and, over the years to get them ingrained in a type? If so, the incentive to classify men for the job they have, or ought to have would become legitimate; and this is where one has to ask whether the three arms of the economic scrummage meet the conditions. Three types of work so alien each to the other as to be not merely different, but different in kind. Ideally different. Antithetic. The ideal divisions of labour which on Baudelairean grounds should throw up three different types of men – *P-cocks, C-chicks, D-kids* – and according to the present thesis, do. Making, when one remembers that the labels carry a good deal more significance than their economic livery suggests, analysis a less sterile exercise than might appear on the surface.

To that we shall come in a minute. Before we do, one thing seems to call for clarification, for on the face of it it does seem slightly ludicrous to categorize men and women as P- or C- or D-types when they are walking models of the three in action. When plainly, man, our hero, is himself a triad, anyway in terms of his own physiology, this would seem to make a nonsense of the whole theory. And certainly does so long as the student neglects to satisfy himself of the obvious; namely that while the three ingredients are standard, the permutations are not. The permutations are infinite; with one constant only in the bias each individual is bound to develop in consequence of his own mix.

This bias will determine his reactions to many matters, albeit not, by any means, all. Occasions there will be when the bias evaporates or to his neighbour's mortification turns up in an unexpected quarter. Hence those inconsistencies of behaviour which while blandly accepted by him so disconcert his friends and enemies. As observed from outside the same man possesses an appearance of wholeness and wholeness being conventionally identified with oneness, inconsistencies of behaviour argue him to be a not-one, a baffling, indeed a disagreeable conception for a fellow citizen disciplined in C-formulae regarding the unities to accept. Admit the personality to be a not-one, a not necessarily well-balanced not-one at that, a not-one whose components may in extreme cases be more than unevenly – ill – matched, or worse, unmatchable; demanding in consequence more than complementary – compensatory – action – at that point the mystery vanishes. Consistency, not its converse, would then become the mystery, even something to distrust, a point made by Tolstoy who maintained that the bona fides of any man whose conduct is unfailingly consistent should be treated with grave suspicion.

P-Cock and C-Chick

We now have a picture of the individual as an economic triplet whose final course of action will revolve eventually round which impulse, productive, consumptive, distributive snatches the scrummager's advantage, the ball. Let us very simply and superficially make an appreciation of these three authors in search of a character, starting with the P-for-producer whose motivation is basically differentiative. Centrifugal, in terms of time and motion; in terms of psychology, emotive. He who occupies the realm of the passions, the religions, the mysteries, the arts, crafts, cults, the negative charge, the masculine gender-signals, these, of the will-to-make, meaning the will-to-be, meaning the will-to-be-different: the productive urge. No quarrel here between art and industry; all positive industrial activities, mass production excepted, have producer affinities, and belong in the last resort to the creative impulse.

At which level the cultist becomes the maker, grower, differentiator of things. The father-figure or P-cock in a marriage whose opposite number, the *consumer* or C-chick, follows different but complementary motivations, gathering unto himself all the identifying routines – law, order, the absolute, universals, wholeness, consistency, gravitation, assimilation, city, civilization, protons, philosophy, the mind, the reason, equality, maths, internationalism, Voltaire, concepts, socialism, communism, totalitarianism, the Corporate State. The world of identity, of Law, of intelligence in its capacity as unifier of all experience may be said to be the C-chick's natural habitat. The born consumer (how well we know him) in every field, cultural, political, economic, he trills always of the processes of law as though mind itself were the creative principle (which it is not); happy only when under the banner of theory he is reducing diversity to identity, the many to the one. Best of all recruits for socialism, or if by birth or education loath to identify himself with reds under the beds, he will still equate political progress with the international egalitarian world. Failing this, the Ivory Tower, a cosy aedicule of his own invention, protected from an anarchist world by an art that is abstract, an architecture which is classic and a God who is one. One, not many, the intellect itself. The monistic Jews with their international outlook, high intellectual and interpretive and low creative capacities, are sometimes claimed to be the racial example of this type; to whom even in religious experience *the Law* takes priority of the *Word* or the *prophets*.

If the same characteristics are typical of most so-called

'cultivated' people today, the explanation is clear enough: for two centuries and more all culture has been associated – wrongly – with the life of the mind, the medium of the identifying impulse whose movement as we have seen is centripetal, a drawing together. Consumptive. The greater the higher. Consumption of TV celluloid, music, architecture, painting, light, heat, games, ceremonial raiment, beer, newsprint, ideas, cosmetics, fashion, company, manners, money. And since consumption takes place at a higher rate in company – since consumption of company is the highest form of consumption – the C-culture is attractive, gregarious, drawing men together, a convener of cities. To which commits himself, foolishly happy, the confirmed C-chick and O how glad thus to spit in the eye of the producer and all his bellyaches, in particular that basic bellyache, agriculture (the 'country'). Instead, huddled cosily behind his city wall (always providing the thing inside the wall *is* a city and not an industrial or commercial camp somewhat disguised) the C-chick earns his keep by juggling with the law, finance, maths, words or similar symbols, representing as they do the measuring, i.e. the identifying, impulse, free so far as any three-dimensional act can be from the productive.

13

THE DISTRIBUTION ECONOMY

The Demon D-Man

Now meet the third member of the triumvirate, offspring of the parental duo but not on that account by any means a model citizen, the demon D-man. D-kid, rather, child of the above marriage – extrovert, physical, games-playing, shower-bath-taking, booby-trapping, practical-joking, always on the way to make a fast buck and as of now dominating the social scrummage. How did this come about? Here one has to go back a bit again. To the Renaissance perhaps, if that title suggests the swapping of the emotive for the rational ideal, implying the rise of sovereign mind, implying amongst other things the *instauratio magna* of Bacon's True Philosophy. Under this new dictatorship contacts were slowly but surely multiplying those conditions of higher communication which in the eighteenth century, with the spread of science both pure and applied and a vast development of the distributive arm, came to a head in the higher organization known as the Industrial Revolution. Which in its turn by hotting up the speed at which goods could be produced, communications developed and contacts made under the pressure of mass production put for the first time the ball at the feet of the distributive arm. For the simplest reasons. He who suddenly increases his turnover a thousandfold will become vulnerable to any task force that will undertake to turn his turnover over. Hence for the first time in history a distribution economy – in general terms capitalism – activated by a new race of entrepreneurs, the task force of D-kids whose energies are dedicated to the arts of distribution rather than, as formerly under scarcity, the battle for goods. Without denying capacity to the producer, the D-arm has set itself by spreading ever wider the distributive network so to hot up that capacity as to put both producer and consumer under permanent obligation. So much so indeed that he, the producer, has ended up practically the hired man, while the conjurors of the distributive trades, by orchestrating publicity and promotion (the media) have succeeded in directing consumer demand to channels of their own choosing in the belief, an odd one to be sure, that the more a society consumes the richer it grows. We are today conditioned at enormous expense to consume liquor, films, tobacco, houses, refrigerators, automobiles, oil, electricity, television, time and miles in ever vaster and vaster quantities, which after all is a way of getting poorer fast. Result, all that we mean by the rise of the middle class to political and economic power, economic imperialism, Adam Smith, free trade, the Liberal party, the bourgeoisie, the *rentier*, the entrepreneur, 'North' as opposed to 'South' in the American Civil War, a Western World hungry for markets where, before, it was greedy for raw materials and ready if needs must to wage war for them – a situation which with the exhaustion of fossil fuels may repeat itself.

No suggestion here that the struggle for production has died down, only that in the developed countries the battle for markets has grabbed the initiative from the battle for raw materials, so that the rugger scrum begins to move compatibly with the new bosses. Progress is now seen as progress, in mass salesmanship (a distributive ploy, we repeat, a D-dodge), whereby a host of people once on the bread-line have been found the means by the wizards of the distributive trades and their financial fairies to acquire more goods and so enable the mass producers to go on turning them out. Under these pressures a proletariat is bound by the logic of events to be kicked upstairs so that it acquires the means (high wages) to become a customer – i.e. consumer, i.e. a member of the club.

Here a qualification must be made. Except in the USA where neither peasantry nor proletariat existed, the Old World, on the pretext that the starving millions of Asia must be provided with products within their means to buy, contrived to combine this New Deal with a policy of low wages. As Marx predicted. Having an un-developed empire to feed and clothe, the British were led in the cause of providing cheap products for the undernourished to undernourish their own providers whose pay-packets were kept light so that the Third World could be cheaply served. In this there is a sort of confused logic but in contradicting the greater logic of a distribution philosophy, which in the cause of the distributive, i.e. mass production, ideals demands heavier pay-packets for all starting with the home front, it sowed the seeds of Britain's later collapse. Low wages defeat inflation (the doppelganger of a D-offensive) but they also deplete the D-philosophy.

Art

From the foregoing the uninitiated might draw the conclusion that the D-arm is made up of none but those unlovely characters by Matthew Arnold dubbed Philistine. This isn't the case. The D-type has its arts and crafts, its poets and painters who, like most Anglo-American artists tend to be Eden-orientated; nature worshippers, that is, nostalgic for their lost innocence, after the manner of Wordsworth, Turner or Whistler, Samuel Palmer, Uvedale Price. Representational art had its source in this materialist (or realist) pool. So too had the movement which swept Europe clean of the whole eighteenth-century ideology of Reason, Gallantry, the Man of Honour, the Man of Taste, substituting in their stead Sentiment, Nature and Galloping Consumption. Much more than a new fad, this, the birth of a radical aesthetic: an anarchist aesthetic; a D-kid aesthetic; involving a revolt that imposed upon the two existing orthodoxies – the Beautiful and the Sublime – a third, a radical, an anarchic, an entropic, a disorderly ideal; the Picturesque. Main stimuli, departures from the norm; a beauty (to use Uvedale Price's favourite word in its deepest sense) of the *irregular* with its renunciation of closed systems and laws-of. According to Payne Knight even a beautiful girl could gain something by the addition of a negligible squint. And though neither Rousseau nor the aristos who allowed themselves to be seduced by him would have seen it that way, this aesthetic of the irregular by placing personal whim above accepted authority or the class sanctions of the Quality, paved the way for a democratic approach to the finer feelings. Another repercussion of the puritan revolution as exemplified perhaps by Sir William Temple who lived through the Protectorate in youth and hardly twenty-five years after Cromwell's death brought irregular gardening to England by way of Chinese picturesque theory known to Sir William as *sharawaggi*. The exact moment perhaps when sensibility became – rather than the product, the rival – of education. The perquisite no longer of the Earl at Court but of the churl at Earl's Court. Who henceforth, in the exercise of his inalienable right as a laws-of renouncer can lay claim to taste, emancipated as now at last that article is from aristocratic midwifery and post-natal treatment. Thus, since *the irregular* makes every man ultimately his own judge of art, Picturesque Theory which fired the first shot of the Romantic movement is a tremendous event in the long apprenticeship of democracy.

For all that, the dominant septs within the D-economy,

loosely identified with the middle classes who thus received the cultural okay, remained then as they do to this day blissfully ignorant of their paternity.

Not of their Deity however. The rise of the D-type to class dominance is clearly documented in the spread of puritanism (God as moral bully, terror of till-pilferers, indispensable disciplinary element in the life of the philosophical anarchist). With the golden handshake going eventually to that Humboldtian, that anarchist, that essentially D-god, who likes his devotees to make a burnt offering of the State on the altar of the individual.

So there they were, the new individualists, middlemen to a man, supremely conscious of independence before their fellows and personal responsibility to their Maker; sentiments that became the watchword of the whole movement. Spilling over into natural philosophy, private enterprise, personal privacy, personal salvation, personal art; and going up with a bang at last in the grand eruption, scientific, economic, political, philosophical, sociological, of the Industrial Revolution and the D-kids' secret weapon, mass production. Password, self-help; or its obverse, laissez faire, fit slogans for a distributive ethic wedded to a philosophy of 'service', the ideal of the ox who treadeth out the corn – on condition he isn't muzzled. Success to the strong leg, the sure hand, the quick eye, ripened in the sports stadium to create a novel form of ballet, grand ritual of D-symbolism: the distribution of a ball. Sometimes one ball, sometimes many balls, but always, by hand, foot, bat, racket, club or cue.

And he is of course still with us in a big way, the demon D-kid, burning up mileage on the by-pass, patronizing its casinos, discotheques, road-houses, tennis courts, clubs, pubs, baths, golf courses, football fields. Populating the suburb, a form of development parasitic upon the city (and civilization) as he, the marketeer of market-towns, once was upon the countryside. Hence, in dedication to his contacts and communications, their alignment along the axis of the routes that carried his machine, cart, coach, carriage or car. Ribbon development: tangled and retangled (but not rectangled).

Thus does the D-kid demonstrate his independence of the P- and C-communities, an *enfant* even more *terrible* than the rest of mankind, being ineradicably *neither – nor*. Neither pro-fugal nor pro-petal, yet, should the whim grab him, pro both; an anarchist whose ethic takes effect but not shape in that two-way bore or race of contrary currents – the commuter wave – scouring out the substance of our cities whichever which way it flows.

Gent

THE SOCIALIST SOCIETY

If you trap the moment before it's ripe
  The tears of repentance you'll certainly wipe.
But if once you let the ripe moment go
  You never can wipe off the tears of woe.
                              William Blake

14
IT'S EARLIER THAN YOU THINK

Back to the Formula

The assumptions of this book are simple. First, that thematic unity or essential concordance must exist between a society and the institutions which reflect its needs, the institution of economics not excepted, where a trinity of parties is spectacularly revealed corresponding to impulses in the nature of man. Notably tortuous as to their higher flights yet down below amongst the grass roots exposing a dialectical framework so simple yet so fruitful in its implications that prediction becomes possible in terms of the three formative principles of the science: production; consumption; distribution. Always remembering that this triumvirate is deputizing for concepts more seminal than the cliché title suggest. Involved, what's more, in a dialogue it is our business to pursue. Because if there is a deadlock and there is, the best bet for its demise lies precisely there – in the dialogue, whose conclusions are designed to resolve it.

So back to the formula and one more effort to decipher what exactly it strives to tell us; in whispers, alas, so dulcet that they pass most of us by. As with less excuse did those more clarion tones of the distributive revolution known to this book as the D-economy.

We are told that there are three antithetic yet reciprocal roles. That the first (P) creates and sells goods (production). That the third in our present order (D) *creates and sells services* (distribution). That the second (C) creates and sells – what? What in the name of surplus value can the consumer create and sell except consumption? Yet how can demand sell that which it is in business to buy? The mind may boggle yet the logic is inexorable. Something there must be for consumption to create and sell and that something can only be consumption. *The consumer creates and sells demand* – or hopes to – and if and when he does succeed, will at last (and virtually for the first time in history) be in a position to dictate his needs to the 'useful and productive classes'. Determine, that is, the utilities he means to extract from the production team and the D-arm and so become at long last the master of the economic infrastructure. Flatly in contradiction to the economic canon. Orthodox theory holds his role as the ultimate source of instruction to be self-evident in virtue of his right to make his demands known. About which all one can say is that whatever the economists hold, to the consumer his role as the source of instruction isn't self-evident nor ever was. For the very good reason that in the unlikely event of his giving that instruction it went unheard. Between them the P- and D-boys were much too busy selling him their ideas to listen to his.

Another example of the gap between theory and practice. Thus in the long haul of history, over shall we say fifty thousand years in the life of economic man, all but 150 can be regarded as a set of variations on the production – that is the scarcity – theme. Not till the rise of natural philosophy, defined today as the scientific spirit and the astounding by-products thereof, of which the Industrial Revolution and its key operation, mass production, was the climactic, need the historian look for an economic upheaval massive enough to be seen as undermining the existing P-economy. Proof, since its preliminary economic cycle is as yet uncompleted, that human history is still waltzing to an early tune. Is indeed so innocent and unsophisticated that confrontation with a revolution as radical as a Distributive take-over left most of its nineteenth-century victims indifferent; while even those, like Marx, who weren't, hailed it as a mere spin-off of the production theme as at first of course it was.

But not for long. So soon as mass production theory gained dominance in the scrummage the initiative, as it was bound to do, changed hands or, rather, feet, so achieving what is justly termed a Distribution economy; whose battalions of D-kids created that brilliant interregnum which by miracles of salesmanship and service brought something like abundance to a huge and hungry sector of mankind. The potential of surplus anyway; a work of philanthropy but also of possible self-destruction, for surplus or even the smell of it is calculated to undermine the claims of this very same elite, whose days on the top of the heap are already numbered, as we now begin to see.

In favour of whom or what?

In favour of the consumer? In favour of the *Consumer society?* With reluctance we draw attention to that phrase, describing as it does precisely what our society is *not*. But ought to be. While conceivably earning its keep as a trend-setter it does nothing more for us or the present debate than horribly confuse the issue. For minute by minute the fact becomes clearer that if a crisis there is, and few will deny its existence, the trouble lies almost certainly in the need for something very different – a consumer *economy*. A new offensive by the second member of the triumvirate to gain the initiative within the scrum; and with it the opportunity to reorientate society's economic life-style. For one department, anyway, a holiday from the rat-race; a change-over-day from life back-here on the D-front to a breath of fresh air on the C-front. To a genuine system break, that is; a break from a D-for-distribution to a C-for-consumer economy with all its adjuncts and implications.

The first of which is revolutionary in that it does exactly what we expect of it by actually provoking a jump from one orbit to another orbit.

From the orbit *poverty* to the orbit *plenty*; from scarcity to surplus; from growth to glut; from a D-kid to a C-chick philosophy; from a seller's to a buyer's market; from a market economy to a consumer economy.

It seems more than likely, indeed certain, that our current hard times in the social, political, and economic fields are a result of this misfortune – *the failure of the consumer economy to make its take-over bid*. The system has been foiled of its break. D-theory remains dominant in an age where another set-up – C-theory and C-chicks – should be making a bid to become within the scrummage primus inter pares.

A take-over bid but, once again, no take-over. No Socialist State. No collectivism. No corporate nonsense. No totalitarian twaddle.

Not to be in too much of a hurry either. More vital to start right rather than quick, in full understanding of the rules of the game, particularly those that govern the economic scrummage – a threesome as we are continually reminded.

For, with whatever good intentions, once the monolithic ideal is conceived to be the logical ideal – and for logic (itself monolithic) the monolithic is always the ideal – once some idiot starts talking about full socialism or total control of the means of production, then, presto, back will crowd our troubles, fruit of the same old errors; with, as per all-out communism (and, come to that, all-out laissez-faire) the same old painful consequences.

Interventionist Chaos

Does this idea of a C-economy really amount to anything that could be construed as a policy for our day and age? How could it not? Though the notion of a mixed economy is already well-established, our problems simply do not have a solution or even the promise of one until the corridors of power open their doors to its implicit challenge. How, namely, to dissipate the fog in which our legislators flounder so long as they continue not to know who, what or where the necessary components of the mixture are. A mixed economy is a singuarly sensible concept, but unless someone decides *how* and *where* to mix it – what mixture to make – what the rules of the mix are – and what the ingredients – it will remain like that crazy kid not so much mixed as mixed up. Worse still, messed up.

This was the mess that haunted Hayeck when he wrote some years ago (in *Individualism & Economic Order*) that what we are doing has no relation to either capitalism or socialism. 'It is necessary to realize that the system under which we live,' he wrote, 'choked up with attempts at partial planning and restrictionism, is almost as far from any system of capitalism which could rationally be advocated as it is different from any consistent system of planning.'

He adds, 'the world of today is just interventionist chaos'. A mixed-up economy in short. Inviting inevitable miscarriage when those of our legislators who manage such affairs neither meet the requirements nor understand the claims of a triple economy. Operative word, *interplay*; which at one stroke removes the notion of a consumer *society* by admitting the existence of the other forces with other objectives, valid even when a consumer *economy* conceives itself to be cock of the walk. As it is, talk of a consumer *society* merely obscures the real situation which involves the creation of a third economy capable of maintaining the C-position against its two partners, a job done in the good old days by Church and Crown – now by Crown alone. The Queen.

Which is why the Queen has to be invited to remain an institution. In a social body dedicated to opportunism and specialization it is natural for the D-kid to treat any investigation of organic principles as a bit of a joke, and so in the D-kid philosophy it is. Now, however, that the D-kids are on the D-skids, the situation rates a closer look, lest, peradventure, in place of the one D-evil we are in the way of casting out (or, rather, slapping down) there enter in (as per the USSR) seven others more deadly than the first.

The lesson is a simple but little respected one, that before a law of any definitive sort finds its way to the statute book the legislator should become the custodian of a certain body of truth concerning the functions of the society he serves. Divisible structurally into the three we have discussed; of which one, the D-kids' miraculous expansion of the market, has affected the course of social history more radically than all the shooting wars and bloody revolutions of two centuries. Making of the sneers of its critics, who in default of the miracle would hardly be there to sneer, a jest.

Let us for thirty seconds dwell on that achievement with the adoration it deserves. Then, loyal genuflections over, it remains to say that the D-economy under whose umbrella the West in the twentieth century has been weathering the new technological challenge is by the very success of its formulae approaching yet another climacteric; and revealing in the process the limitations of its brief, founded as that is on the identification of progress with a perpetually expanding economy. Or, to say the same thing in reverse, the concept of scarcity. Conceive of an end to scarcity or even a rift between growth and progress and the growth economy vanishes together with the whole D-philosophy. Conventional D-economic thought included, rooted as both are in the concept of shortage. Nothing terrifies the orthodox economist more than the idea of abundance – i.e. surplus. With good reason. Were it to become persistent our whole way of life would seize up in bank failures, credit freezes, defaulting debtors, unemployment, industrial bankruptcy, commercial collapse. On a scale so grandiose that as a working discipline the practice of economics in its present form would fold.

On the other hand, assuming as one has to that when fossil fuels fail, man will be spry enough to nobble free energy, solar, tidal or what have you, (methane, hydrogen), the automative and cybernetic probabilities in an open society are all in favour of glut and a technology of abundance; so that the question 'whither society?' becomes a burning, or perhaps one should say a silicon, one. Because unless abundance can be reconciled with an economic philosophy of more pith and moment than that which now troubles us the conventional Western way of life is going to come unstuck even more seriously than its worst enemies believe.

An early-warning system against the ultimate catastrophe is at this very moment turning in upon the chain of EEC food and wine lake-mountains locked away in icy fortresses scattered throughout Europe and its off-shore island.

15

FIRST INDENT: SELLING DEMAND

Leisure

If for argument's sake the foregoing is so far admitted as to make a C-economy acceptable to the twentieth century (or supposing we are tardy enough, the twenty-first) the burning question becomes: what form should this *ingressio*, this *instauratio magna* take?

Here no alternative decently presents itself but a return yet again to the formula which suggests as we have seen that the individual is involved in a deal with the State by which he makes his demands known; while the State on its side undertakes to buy them in return for his services. He *sells* his needs and *gives* his services (the converse of D-practices), replenishing thereby the resources of his property (the State) to the point where aided by EEC food mountains and wine lakes it can find the means to buy his demands or in another odd figure of speech – furnish his wants.

A play on words? Naturally. Any sort of analysis, including the rigorous expositions of the ordinary language philosophers, involves a play on words if only because it is the nature of words to play. To play games. Whether by failing to say ··hat they mean or failing to mean what they say. Worse, to grow more ambiguous, more ambivalent, more inconsequential, more fallible, the harder they are pressed to yield their meaning or lack thereof. In the games playing words of Niels Bohr, 'language is not describing facts but creating images', an opinion that would have warmed the heart of Wittgenstein. The real issue is whether in consequence of such word-play, matters are to be seen in a more suggestive light; for it should be pretty clear by now that words change their allegiance according to the economy they reflect, not to mention the context they serve; not to mention the mouth they come out of. Not to mention the ear-drum they offend. Anyone who tries to harness words to a constant or even consistent meaning must be either a don or a bit of an ass. Two different articles let us hasten to say. Not only trained but paid to treat words as suspect, dons behave towards them, very properly, in the manner of a prosecuting counsel cross-examining a villain of the criminal underworld.

Take, for example, 'leisure'. At first glance the term suggests undoing the top trouser button, relaxing, putting the feet up; a misrepresentation, as Lord Fortinbras, that selfless public servant, demonstrated. Even when 'leisure' is used as a synonym for 'pleasure' it still remains a fact that for the leisured classes most of it is spent furiously chasing inedible animals or incalculable women or just balls. Thus whatever the distinction is between 'busy-ness' and 'business' or, if you like (it would be just as logical), 'leisure' and 'pleasure,' it isn't whatever is at issue between 'work' and 'idleness' or 'activity' and 'inertia'. In fact, the difference lies purely and simply in being paid for one and not the other. A person is paid because in one case he is held to be adding to the wealth of society; he is not paid because in the other he is held to be merely enjoying the fruits thereof – that is, consuming or abetting the consumption of this wealth.

Which is where at last the basic distinction grins through. What else are 'business' and 'leisure' than synonyms for the distributive and consumptive impulses. While no actual stigma attaches to the idea of leisure, too much – meaning more than a little – isn't considered quite nice. *Laborare est orare.* Short rations for most of us as soon as we indulge more than is thought desirable by our masters or betters in one at the expense of the other; followed by *unemployment*, another confused word. The only kind of business one dare expect to be paid for is the P- or D-kind. Goods and services. C-business being regarded as counter-productive, leisure quickly becomes idleness and, actively pursued, conspicuous waste. Fair enough in a scarcity economy, where our hero, insofar as he is a consumer, must first make or distribute the goods he wants to get outside of.

The question is, is it always fair enough – is it an ethical or an economic imperative? Austere moralists who insist that it is not good that man should consume his pleasures in idleness have long been accepted as the proper guides in these matters, yet leisure as we have seen, is not idleness and the morality that regards it as such a scarcity, a P- or D-morality, whose uses in a world of mass production and atom power (plenty) is dubious. Even if work is good for the soul, there is nothing to say unpaid – that is C-work – that is the frenzy of energy we put into our hobbies – is bad for the soul just because one is paid and the other isn't. We are not taught even by the most prickly of puritans that paid work alone is good for the the soul.

The point is laboured here because half – some would say all – our economic morality is relative. Springs from the necessity of the case rather than from any absolute standard of behaviour. The stigma against the name of idleness in the sense we have used the word 'leisure', belongs entirely to this form of contingent morality. And undergoes instant transmogrification when re-interpreted in hard – rather than good – luck terms as unemployment. A play on words if ever there were one, suggesting that the chap involved is *out of work,* (another deceptive phrase), whereas no one until he goes through the front door feet foremost is either.

What the words purport to mean we all naturally know, conditioned as we are to accept no act as an act of *work* unless and until one gets paid for it; the scarcity concept again, wished on us by P- and D-philosophers. Better far to see work under surplus and a C-economy as a job you do for free: a contribution to the club which in return 'buys' – that is to say agrees – your reasonable demands and sets out to provide them. A ratio there will have to be between man-hours of work and the available commodities, with vouchers to prove it, and these could be described as money by such pedants as could and almost certainly would go on to point out that however you phrase the idea it comes down in the end to precisely the same thing: bartering your work for goods.

But this is where surplus and scarcity theory part company, for unlike the conditions under a market economy where you have to take what others provide or go without – work out how many newly-weds have currently to go without a home – under a C-for-Surplus economy you merely state your requirements – *sell* your demands – and get your house in return for two years work at 35 hours a week. All this without prejudice to the demands of the private sector where (in case you are getting nervous) working hours, remember, will be growing progressively shorter year by year. Whether those two years and 35 working hours are spent on the wards of the local hospital or with a Co-op actually building the house is incidental except insofar as one way you will have to wait – two years – and the other you will (hopefully) get the property on the HP by return of post. Either way your reasonable demands are met, while in the former case you, for your part, are working to satisfy the reasonable demands of one of your neighbours. To a scarcity addict this probably sounds mad enough but as the event will prove it makes rather good sense. All this revolution requires, and a revolution it is, is a new attitude to national service – the C-economy – socialism to some – the Crown – the Queen to others – besides certain adjustments to the existing set-up which we must now discuss. Before we do, however, let us take a quick glance at the present situation of welfare and social security; tentative C-exercises but, as the present argument understands it, carried out in ignorance of the C-philosophy that underlies them. Starting with the dole, a practice that flouts every principle of public as well as private economic morality by in effect empowering the man of leisure to levy taxation on the worker. Pure victimization of the useful citizen by the useless – with no criminal intent on the part of the latter, himself a victim, whose dilemma, however, exemplifies in its own person the incapacity of existing economic orthodoxies to deal with society's most crucial problem.

The cure? A very simple one. *To create a new economic situation.* One under which when private enterprise falters, the new deal, rather than clobbering the old, can provide an alternative life-style under national service – like national hunt – rules. He who under private enterprise is thus rendered redundant transfers temporarily or permanently – the choice is his – to State or local authority employment which sets out to provide him with a basic but satisfying way of life. Under such management wealth will no longer provide an incentive worth remorseless pursuit. The 'rich' in a P-economy would stock-pile other men's man-hours into 'banks' in order to be able to sell their own demands to themselves. Under a C-economy, when the objective of the good life can be comfortably realized by machinofacture, satisfaction of reasonable demands as a must for all will, anyway for the C-chick, make 'wealth' tautological.

Unintelligible even. Anyone is wealthy whose reasonable demands are realized and these can now be chalked up in man-hours. And since under the rules of national service it is inconvenient to try to stock-pile the man-hours of others, the issue between you and your powers of consumption resides simply on the amount of service outside the private sector you are prepared to offer the nation.

Obviously the Welfare State is already some way along the C-road, though, to repeat again, not so far as those believe who speak glibly of the consumer society. *That,* with its appropriate economy is, as we have seen, still awaiting the revolutionary rethink in semantics that will undermine the present meaning of words like 'work', 'leisure', 'profit', 'loss', 'wages', 'property', 'wealth', 'employment', 'unemployment', 'service'. The system is, nevertheless, virtually operational today and would be proving its worth already had our legislators not set up the whole package under the wrong title deeds, the price one has to pay for the conventional wisdom. Still, while simple in essence the issue involved in a revolution of this sort can involve complications only the specialist is trained to handle, so here we stick by the basic guide-lines, leaving the details to be dealt with later; on which pretext we ask the reader to treat the present recommendations less as a summary of particular reforms than as symptomatic of the kind of rethink a system break of this calibre invites.

The inescapable conclusion is that under a consumer economy the individual must occupy ground where he can make his wants (or needs) known to the authorities, while they, the authorities – the crucial point, this – *must* in return for his offer to work in the nation's service without pay, be under obligation to provide them. The bureaucracy already fructifying under Social Security and Welfare would be the obvious instrument for the job, with or without the more hierarchic organization provided by local, county, regional, central, authority. But however it works the individual must remain the source of instruction by reason of his right to make his demands known. Small demands to begin with but with the growth of the organization an ever expanding flow of goodies.

16
SECOND INDENT: AN ALTERNATIVE CURRENCY

Domestic Needs and Global Currencies

At what point then does the new economics take over from the old?

At no point. There is to be no take-over. The old economics is still well equipped to look after most of the current needs of the human animal. Only where the private sector and the profit motive fall down on the job, there only do we now expect the State – the C-state – you and me – to move in on the D-kids with a bid for authority in the name of national service. The Queen v. Private Enterprise. Fair enough. But having moved in do we take over the other team's philosophy? Surely not. Do we take over its objectives? Surely not. Do we take over its economic policy? Surely not. Do we take over its money? Surely not. If the target of a consumptive economy is tangental to that of a distributive economy; if its policy seeks satisfaction for the C-chicks rather than profits for the D-kids; if it has no serious intention of making profits or money at all, why then think in terms of profits or money? Why bother about *having* or using money – in particular D-money? A currency? Well . . . global monetary policy covers global needs and the globe is the globe and unto the globe must be rendered that which is the globe's. Nothing here, on the other hand, to suggest that global needs should render invalid a domestic currency covering domestic needs, or that the domestic currency covering domestic needs must be tied as a matter of course to the global currency covering global needs. Another of those myths that need to be quietly strangled, the conventional wisdom that accepts as given the concept that one currency and one only can properly have currency. Different currencies there have been, are, and always will be; and circumstances exist in which such are useful things to have. The trouble starts when custom dictates a standardized course of action.

Money is simply a means of exchange and if you can't or won't exchange goods and services with another party, parish, corporation, county, country or continent, nothing is gained by using a common coinage. A closed system is often a convenience and its fans may get on better by using a means of exchange not exposed to external pressures. Cigarettes, for instance, the German currency after the last war; or cheese in parts of Southern Italy; or the coca leaf demanded today as wages by the native Peruvian Indians whose slimming exercises are built around a diet of cocaine. Or for the Australian supermen in the early days of the colony, very typically, rum. Why not for the new consumer economy an alternative currency tied in no visible way to pound, dollar, franc, mark, or rouble? Two economic life-styles, distributive and consumptive, with two currencies that provide a certain independence for each by offering the citizen two concurrent standards of life, means of livelihood, kinds of money, scales of value. One home-grown, nitty-gritty, grass roots stuff, a sort of basic English style, grounded in national service and so far as humanly possible confined to the UK's internal capacity to provide a T-shirt culture – operating automatic import controls. The other – 'commerce' – the D-kid Spectacular – carrying as it does now the burden of exports, communications and world trade.

There would of course have to be a tie-up somewhere but that could be a secret buried deep within the icy heart or darkened vault of some ultimate auditor.

Unlikely Monies

Again, nothing new here. Crackpot amateurs have dabbled in currency management since economics became a sport; so have many highly qualified professionals, the Douglasites, and in the Thirties the Dutch economist Professor Gondrian (*How to Stop Deflation*) with arguments later elaborated by two unrelated Grahams (Benjamin of New York, Frank D. of Princeton), who showed how a commodity reserve currency could be created by means so simple and workmanlike that even the ranks of Tuscany, or anyway the house of Hayek, could scarce forbear to cheer. Issued solely in exchange against a fixed combination of warehouse warrants for a number of storable raw commodities and redeemable in the same commodity unit, this currency was worked out for national adoption by the US Government under what would have been a closed wartime economy. The raw commodities on which the Graham Plan was based were five grains, four fats and oilseed, three other foodstuffs, four metals, three textile fabrics, tobacco, hides, rubber and petrol. Complicated by the sound of it, but we have Hayek's word that the scheme would in fact be so simple to operate that much of the work could be left to private initiative.

However, this is not the place to go into details which can only be properly debated by the specialist. All one needs to do here is to point out the magical consequences that could attend the effective establishment of a reserve currency operational on the home front where foreign cars, television sets or Vodka would themselves be reserved – for the rats of the rat-race – and standards of living plummet to a level far below the ethos of the stockbroker belt with beer and country wines and home-produced pasta (some of it admirable).

But isn't this exactly what many of us want, the honour of second-class citizenship, already in demand by the coming generation, many of whom are not the turn-on-get-loaded-drop-outs of the reject fraternity, but stern young performers who find their elders full of wind? Always remembering that there will still be two classes, two systems, two currencies, two standards,* one, home-grown but equal to all serious emergencies; the other, the existing order, where the D-kids dance to their own tune. Such a division of labour would surely crystallize the functions and pin-point the area of operation of the public sector, channelled as its activities will then be towards objectives outside the market system's proper capacities or real interests.

Do alternative currencies create problems? Of course. Insoluble ones according to the conventional wisdom. But if it calls for one at all a C-for-consumption economy demands, as we maintain, a currency other than that serving the P- and D-arms because amongst other things when theirs falters a running mate is there to take the strain.

What form would it have? Can the Establishment really be expected to embark on so unscrupulous an adventure? Why not? Far from accepting the idea as novel the public can remind its masters that alternative currencies have generally existed and today still do. There are plenty of institutions which work within what might be called the Green Shield syndrome, the kibbutz for example, where members of the community work for

*For ease of argument the third (more accurately, first) – the P- culture has been ignored throughout this debate on the grounds of its familiarity.

free in return for an issue of vouchers at the end of the month exchangeable for goods in the farm store. Pedants may still maintain that this comes down to the same thing, work for pay, but there is a difference they ignore in that the vouchers are not standard currency; are negotiable only within a closed system. If they are money they are domestic money, and if we are forced to concede the case for an alternative currency the question arises whether a C-economy might not call for exactly that.

17
THIRD INDENT: PRIVATE WORKS

Bottom-up Strategy

Where does the new system differ from the old? In an unusual, even unexpected way. When price and planned economies, planning and market systems, public and private sectors, reveal so many characteristics in common – ultimate profit is after all the objective of all and the excercise of long-term planning, certainly not the monopoly of one – the amateur may be forgiven for wondering whether their differences are quantitative rather than qualitative. Another characteristic they have in common, a poor power to weight ratio, enormous power but at the cost of so much *avoirdupois* that we, the puny authors of both systems, can hardly be said to have a hand in either. Multi-national corporations, conglomerates, public works, welfare state, nationalization (a third of all industry) involve a bureaucratic organization beside which the petty interests of the individual count scarcely at all. Theory maintains that this juggernaut operates in his interest, a useful idea and one that might soften the humiliation were the results as useful as the idea. However, when every attempt to put the heat into industry or plan the economy from the top down ends in bizarre failure he might prefer a build-up nearer his own end of the business on what has been called a bottom-up strategy – small after all *is* beautiful. To maintain that the impulse to look after the little man is foreign to the bureaucratic ideal would be unjust as Welfare demonstrates, yet its cost to the community proves that the execution or rather the philosophy (deficit financing not-withstanding) is faulty. Nothing can be given for nothing. Given, yes, but in return for another gift – service – demanded even from OAPs, many of whom feel dead and buried and would welcome exhumation.

Money? Within the current meaning of the act, none, or, if convenience dictates, some voucher-style medium of exchange, none that can be hung on to any kind of existing currency. A C-economy demands, as we have seen, a private one, small and beautiful and holding good only within the ambience of the C-arm, whose gifts will come (hopefully) 80% within the domestic sector, leaving a taxable liability only on those commodities which cannot be supplied therein. You give your services to the State which in return buys your demands, and the amount it buys will depend on the work you are prepared to clock up under whatever system of accountancy obtains. Almost any system will do so long as it remains apparently unrelated to pounds and pence.

The conception is so naive that it may appear simple-minded. All one can say is that if the idea of working for the community for free is dotty what is one to make of the existing practice known as social security (the dole) which consists of *not* working for the community on a salary. More novel anyway, for while all societies have looked with disfavour on what used to be called pauperization, the practice of free-labour for the community, as we shall later try to demonstrate, has a long history, an army of addicts, or adepts, a well-proven philosophy, and a record of solid though hardly unqualified success.

Here no more is claimed than that the practice should be given a wider base on the grounds that in the event, virtually all our current frustrations would crumble, revealing our position as what it really is, impregnable. Competition between public and private sectors there will of course be, but little throat-cutting by rivals whose appeal is to a different arm of the public, one status-seeking, the other (from principle rather than necessity) status-fleeing. National Service: the only real meaning the word *socialism* ever had, long practised within the military Establishment by officers of the State whose blood pressure spirals at the mere mention of the politics they operate (the knifing of this service under the Macmillan dispensation was the political crime of the era). Developed to include virtually the total range of national activities, it will make unemployment meaningless and social security meaningful. When one area of the market economy hits the D-skids the other will take over on the C-front, enabling the citizen to switch as occasion demands from one kind of service to another, or better still put in part-time on both, a practice automation and cybernetics not to mention microchips will eventually dictate.

With this one long-overdue reform a C-economy can be expected to make its debut under rather unexpected conditions; nothing less than a rebirth of private in the field of public initiative. The opportunity, that is, to reverse the conventional picture of socialist con- versus private nonconformity. And under the consumer's right to make his own demands known, a new opportunity for personal initiative outside the progressively more authoritarian and megalomaniac market sector, where under the current bureaucracy of capitalism private enterprise, let's face it, does seem in danger of being strangled by private enterprise.

Bottom-up Strategy

And this, precisely, is the opportunity a C-economy will provide, a bottom-up strategy, based on the principle that before our masters decide who does what (the planning system) or who does who (the market system) they must at last accept the first premise of the science (never in fact realized) that *demand must be initiated by the individual*, who is the ultimate source of instruction by reason of his right to make his demands known. The consumer credo: to be realized by a C-economy where the State has at last the obligation to 'buy' his, the individual's, demands. Upon which foundation all future enterprise in the public sector should be built: the bottom-up philosophy, serving what can reasonably be called a socialist ideal, yet by one of those ironies of politics that sometimes please the cynic committing planning policy to the amplification of the little man's freedom of choice. At the moment, too, when over-involvement in planning is bureaucratizing capitalist as well as socialist practice, crippling its privacy, its freedom and its enterprise. The current Frankenstein: bureaucracy; somehow, despite those bulging biceps, to be warned off all totalitarian dreams of power, an addiction like drink, and, like drink, a tyranny. Attainable only by a steely resolve on the part of public opinion – conspiracy if you like – to type-cast the State as a resourceful mother figure and see that it acts as such, rather than an am-I-or-am-I-not-master-in-my-own-house male despot. Privilege and power against sheer weight of numbers and here the numbers must win. Alexander von Humboldt, first of the scientific explorers and father of modern geography who in 1799 discovered curare and electric eels during his 1,500 mile exploration of the Orinoco, maintained that head hunters, cannibals, starvation, fever and all other jungle perils were secondary evils compared with the persistent day-long attack by gnats that made life on a canoe heading for the Amazon a living hell. A gnat and the little man have one thing in common: magnitude – in the sense that though relatively insignificant on their own, they are excessively numerous. They come in swarms, a fact of life they must now learn to use on Humboldt the bureaucrat.

Humboldt the bureaucrat, as every functionary does, will start by banging away at his persecutors in the hope that the little beasts will get tired and steer for easier game. But when faced with the stark reality, that he, their chosen prey, is a prisoner in his own Town Hall surrender will then be only a matter of time, and victory for gnats, individually contemptible, collectively irresistible, assured. The one condition, this, in which a bureaucracy, Humboldtian or otherwise, can be tolerated.

Nor is the bureaucrat the only party whose authority will be in question. The mandate to withhold labour of those capitalist institutions the Trade Unions can hardly run under a C-economy since such action would merely victimize the rank and file striker whose access to welfare, social security and OAP must be (except for the sick) dependent on his willingness to do his bit for the State (in the private sector his and his Union's rights remain of course unchanged).

Nor is this the only delicate issue to be negotiated under a consumption economy. In a system break of this nature any sane politician will approach the problems involved with a proper discretion. Even more crucial, however, is the capacity to understand what the new set-up is in aid of, and at this point it becomes vital to have a clear picture of the principle dictating the action. In lieu of a principle to follow, action of any sort becomes meaningless, indeed dangerous, possibly disastrous; exactly the situation forced on the nationalization programme, an insane mopping up of large-scale industries unaided by any principle higher than the itch to knock capitalism off its perch. Not just insane, suicidal, with, immanent in the exercise, the collapse of the whole scrummage. To repeat once again, all we need to do with free enterprise is leave it alone, turning to national service (not socialism) to provide under the Crown the new dynamic needed by the body social. An offensive that will render unemployment itself redundant, the word as well as the thing. Both will go; first the thing, unemployment – out of circulation; finally, the word *unemployment* – out of mind. To become, when each citizen works automatically for more than one master a load of unintelligible gibberish which in years to come fathers will be at a loss to explain to their offspring. That happy event will herald other happy ones including the return of 'repairs', the end of inflation and a vast drop in taxation.

18

FOURTH INDENT: WORKING FOR FREE

Despite anything just said, there will be sceptics who consider the whole concept of (1) *working for free* a piece of prevarication as great as, though no greater than, (2) *selling demand*. Before the critic dismisses either notion as raving lunacy he must be warned that (1) is in operation at this moment, indeed has been going strong for centuries under what might be called a consumer morality. Not, it's true, a faith free from all stain since it has long been held in suspicion, but one that according to the argument of this book will eventually win world-wide acceptance for the new economic philosophy.

If (1) isn't a new economic concept, (2) as we have seen already happens to be as old as the science itself – its first precept and principle indeed – founded as we have seen on the consumer's mission to 'instruct' the producer re his needs: selling his demands, in other words.

However, as we have also seen, this doctrine was an idealization of a situation which was largely imaginary; so imaginary, in fact, as to justify our presenting it as a radical innovation. It is not, however, entirely unknown. There is an example of a C way of life operating within our own society. For century upon century, unsuspected by others, a group of men have been practising the C-gospel. Demonstrating by the most persuasive means of all, example, that the consumer economy is something more than a piece of line-shooting invented for the specious purposes of this book. Here, on the contrary, is a living conspectus of beliefs, with an august history, a hero of its own, a plot of its own, an ethos, an economy, a morality of its own. You may approve or disapprove but there it is and there it has been for longer than memory can measure, growing moment by moment more significant for current economic philosophy.

Unacknowledged, as the matter is understood here, only because the disguise it wears invites the prejudices that gang up on the concept of class. Maybe one should say *a* class, in this case a sept or order that has always worked in the public cause free of charge. For which ingenious economic sharp-practice its solo performer was awarded the title gent or *man of leisure*.

A *gentleman*. He who deigns to live like any other man but not by *earning a living*. He who refrains from doing a service for pay by doing ditto for no pay – none at least but such as appears to come out of his own private purse and personal economic system. Who on the strength of that act of altruism has installed himself and his peers as a perpetual governing class and in the persons of the squirearchy, the stately homers, ministers, JPs, C of Es, proceeds to govern for nothing those of us who can't afford the privilege of working for nothing. The C of E tradition, no longer operative of course, was typical. A consumer in Holy Orders was privileged to sell his consumptive demands, i.e. 'right' to a 'living', by appropriating 10% of all his flock's production. In return he looked after their immortal requirements free of charge.

This, then, is the argument. That the title to gentility, traditionally associated with those privileged people who have no need to soil their hands with honest work is – in all its aspects and branches, its bias for 'leisure', its concentration on sport (not sports: these are D-routines), its passion for consumptive rather than productive or distributive work (shooting for instance), for 'unearned' rather than 'earned' income; and finally, its preoccupation with those consumer techniques known to the rival philosophy as conspicuous waste – is no more and no less than the traditional C-ethic. The gentleman is the embodiment of the C-culture.

Hard Leisure

One is speaking of course of the past. Some jobs brought in remuneration of a sort if only by monopolies or bribery but these were fringe benefits. Except for the clergy each of the people involved, challenged to say what he *did*, would say he didn't *do* anything, and his way of running the country was in fact far from arduous. His leisure on the other hand was mostly hard – hard leisure – indistinguishable except in the impulse that bred it from hard labour – the hunting down of wild and dangerous animals from the saddles of animals even more dangerous. And, after the capture or slaughter thereof, dangerous coach-journeys to Westminster to prevent the tenantry, that constant danger, doing likewise on threat of deportation or the rope.

To dwell on his eccentricities, however, would be far from just. The gent who didn't *do* anything did create a wonderfully civilized life-style, agreeable, useful, creative, organic, gracious, healthy and manly. In peace he worked at perfecting it; in war he led his men into battle entreating them not to want to live for ever and setting them the example. Not really a dull moment for this top person who only refused 'work' in the accepted financial sense because, having already salted enough away to make his disdain of money a status symbol, he could sell his demands to his own estate. A gentleman of leisure would, while working for nothing, remunerate himself for this act of conspicuous waste; and it is good to be able to record that he was big-hearted about the cost, complaining not at all of the debts that came winging their way in.

The gentleman toils not, neither does he spin. He has been called a drone, he has been called a parasite. He has been called the man who won't soil his hands with honest work. For centuries (it has weakened now) the distinction was this very curious, almost one might say bizarre one, between the man of leisure (private means, gent) and the man of trade (money grubber). To be a gent you had to be a drone and any gent who went 'into trade' lost his status, just as any tradesman who wanted to become a gent had to come out of trade. Later, he had to express this renunciation geographically, by leaving the city. Thus the *country* gentleman. Only citizens had their roots in the city. The gentleman was no citizen and the citizen was no gentleman.

Trade, you notice – commerce – the D-game. No such taint attached to the P-game. The rents you took from your farms or the profits from merchant adventures didn't involve personal labour – were in fact hang-overs from the original producer economy. So long as you didn't go down it you could even own a mine.

Today, when peers are advertising agents or car-salesmen and tradesmen retire to their country seats to jiggle with horses, guns and pedigree herds, it might be thought that the tradition had ceased to operate. Closer inspection shows that while the characters switch parts the distinction remains clear enough to be seen as a contest between two antithetic philosophies, one distributive, the other consumptive. Under the new economy every member of the race can hardly expect to be a lord of the manor if only because manors are by now in short supply; also in current social morality not to have or appear to have a job is bad form.

Yet the image curiously enough remains the same; of the gentleman, who is a country gentleman, if only of the week-end cottage or stockbroker belt, living (weekends) to all appearances in 'idleness' until the bell tolls Mondays when early risers catch him sneaking to some secret rendezvous his wife and family have hardly seen or scarcely heard of and none but his fellow commuters are free to name.

Curtains to all that business of living over the shop. Idleness is, of course, the wrong term, as Nancy Mitford wittily demonstrated in the person of Lord Fortinbras* whose life of violent activity, some of it useful, amounts in the eyes of the world to doing nothing merely because he never was nor ever expected to be paid; he being able under his own private economic system to sell such demands as he had to himself. Accordingly he is free to spend his days in public work or charitable enterprises, thus achieving an early ruin. In this gentleman's progress Miss Mitford identifies the essential economic characteristic of the breed more aptly than we by the remark that effort in his view is not so much unpaid as *unrelated* to money. Fortinbras is on the go from morn to night, but it is a go that pays no dividends since it and the profit motive were never identified in his mind. However hard up and literally far-from-home this aristocrat gets in his progressive bankruptcy one thing never occurs to him – to *earn* a living. The idea that one *sells* effort in order to *make* money doesn't enter into his calculations.

To the wage slave such innocence smells of degeneracy. Nothing of the sort; Fortinbras is a man of high energy and excessive public spirit. He kills himself with overwork in the cause of others, and except for the army pay that comes to him in the war through what might be called a bureaucratic accident, never sees the inside of another's cheque book. He could of course afford his altruism only because his forbears had been acquisitive in a way that is no longer open to most of us. To most of us the present prospect is more likely to be a waiting-list for a council house – already the stately home of a third of all Englishmen. Nevertheless we are, through Parliament, collective owners of another even larger Estate – the State – and this could provide many basic commodities and services – in particular *services* – without prejudice to either the D- or P-economies. To its rivals' advantage, indeed, since the closed system a C-economy would have to operate on an alternative currency involves auto-

---

Noblesse Oblige (Hamish Hamilton).

matic import controls, and for that and other reasons a huge improvement in the balance of payments. Goodbye to inflation too.

On paper the pedant is free to maintain that either way the sense is the same, but if the sense is the same the priorities are not, which is precisely where the difference lies – in the order of priorities. The ideal of work unrelated to money has more mileage than the ideal of the wage-slave unelated by work.

Here we come to the nub and crux of this operation: nothing less than a fresh initiative designed to invent a code that dispenses with not merely the existence *the idea* of unemployment. Paid *idleness*, once called pauperization, is today called *unemployment*; work, so long as it is unpaid, *leisure*. Suppose we substitute leisure for unemployment and call its operator a consumer or C-chick in the interest of whom the State (the public equivalent of the private estate) sets out to provide his basic needs free. One condition and one condition only is imperative: that the State should not run out of goods and services. Hence we make a circle by offering some – in the case of the otherwise 'unemployed', all – of our leisure to the State and so make the operation viable and so divorce work from orthodox money. Work/goods could not in the event go wholly unrelated but the tie-up could be kept in purdah within the operations room of some Ministry of Furtive Tricks.

Thus the Estate, a public one held collectively by all, could be made to provide goods and services in ratio to the free work put into it under the terms of a consumer economy. Gentility in the old sense doesn't arise. Nonetheless the identification of the principle with the classes who have already applied it for centuries does, when carried out under the eye of a private citizen for his own C-convenience, indicate how amenable a consumption philosophy can be. How to widen the options and so achieve a consumer culture is all that remains; no longer private and personal but collective, embracing the whole citizenry, gents to a man.

Here we must rely on the general public themselves who, having no private resources but the State, which has no resources of any sort bar them, must be prepared to invest their capital (i.e. brains and brawn) in their joint property, in the form of services which will make that property resource-ful. With, by another of those ironies that abound in this area of politics, consequences that will give the little man, squeezed at present between the twin millstones of monopoly capitalism and the bureaucracy of the public sector, some control over both, by virtue of his ability under the new economy to *instruct* market and planning systems in his needs. Suddenly and without warning, presto, individual initiative, private enterprise; a very unexpected socialist consequence.

Remembering always that in working for free (leisure) the gent is practising what the political bosses of a consumer economy should preach. Why? Why do the ideals of the gentleman and the consumer society coincide? There can be only one answer: because the life-style of the one is the philosophy of the other. The C-chick has followed his policies and practices since civilization was born, exposing them to the hostile gaze of prophets (like Marx) who aimed to liquidate him in the name of a consumer gospel he, the gent, had initiated and still seeks to perfect.

No crisis. Or if there is it is self-inflicted. In terms of the rugger scrum, the initiative is passing from one set of forwards, the D-kids, to another, the C-chicks; in no way an anxious moment unless, as the weight tells against them, the losing side, rather than gracefully reversing, over-reacts by over-resistance, so collapsing the scrum. Disastrous, this, to the whole outfit since in the absence of a counterweight the heavier men will themselves collapse on those they have collapsed.

Total collapse. If there is a crisis, this is it: ignorance of the rules of the game. Leading the D-arm to turn and fight when it should be giving way; and tempting the C-arm, big-headed with success, to plot a take-over of the D-kids that will destroy the organic structure of the triumvirate.

Chick

THE ALTERNATIVE SOCIETY

Nothing in the world is more powerful than an
idea whose time has come.

Victor Hugo

19
THE ALTERNATIVE SOCIETY

The Crisis of Crisis

We have now arrived at the moment when the lines of thought so far developed need to be laid alongside; on the presumption, far-fetched no doubt, that whatever underlying coherence there is in the general argument will have them, not merely running parallel, but in the great perspective of history gravitating to a point. Here in the specialist's interest one ought to make a distinction between professional and amateur forms of the sport. On wage drift or cash squeeze or money supply or Phillip's curve no one really wants to listen to the lay-brother who isn't equipped to make contributions of interest in that league. The specialist on the other hand is by definition debarred – indeed debars himself – from plotting grand strategy, his suspicion of which rubs off alas on the politicians who go to him for advice on this very issue, strategy, and come away determined to do without it. Absolute nonsense of course; in the absence of a strategy the war is lost before it begins and so is the habit, also denigrated by the specialists, of public debate, trademark of a parliamentary democracy and silly or not the mark of a healthy one. Replete with possibilities moreover. Specialization has won famous victories but its impulse to stifle all but the received opinion rubber stamped by the presiding élite is totally unacceptable and must always be challenged by any democrat worthy of his amateur status. Statesmen remain amateurs too and to their eternal credit admit it, and in that respect are loaded like juries with the responsibility for giving a verdict on the strategy they lean over backwards to evade.

As to this present debate it has to be admitted – with particular reluctance as we have already said – that at the point now reached the oft repeated warning against taking crisis for real is becoming more and more difficult to sustain. Humiliating for an argument which has consistently stressed the non-existence of any genuine trouble but when one looks at all the real trouble in fact there is, our planet seems not so much crisis-prone as crisis proven. And some part of this one has to accept if only because to ignore its existence now isn't going to bring consolation to those who suffer the consequences; or confidence in the argument to those who count the costs. Michael Shanks for one, whose latest book* lists some of the terrors that threaten the permissive society, from little creepy ones – electronic bugging, Taylorism, shop floor alienation, manning levels, excessive noise et al – to the real monsters, the all-but-fatal body-blows – trade union confrontation with Government, cost-push inflation (exemplified by OPEC), the end of full employment, the internal contradictions of capitalism (foretold by Marx), repressive police states, State ideology, the shadow of totalitarianism; the Mafia State with the growing incidence of hijacks, muggings, kidnapping, hooliganism, vandalism and large-scale crime, polarization between rich and poor, low labour costs in the Third World, stress symptoms arising from over-concentration of population, the Club of Rome's unsustainable population growth (England is the most crowded country on earth). Such monumental headaches as bureaucracy, institutionalization, giantism, multi-national and multi-product conglomerates are eclipsed by a monumental nightmare, nuclear weaponry. Most sinister of all, the world population explosion (4,000 million, doubling every 35 years – 8,000 million by AD 2010). Despite which the race has so far managed to squeeze itself into no more than 12% of the earth's surface.

Idiotic on the face of it to suggest that these and a hundred more imbroglios could be susceptible to one grandiose cure-all. Clearly the problems cover a huge area of social relations and if there are solutions they will be of a highly complex kind. Economic measures may contribute to but can't be expected to find a remedy for what is basically a crisis of society. So says Michael Shanks, like any other man of reason.

And yet . . .

And *yet* . . . when all the either-ors are said, let the reader cast his eyes over each of these enormities in turn, then, if he dares, consider without prejudice one way or the other how all but the population explosion would fare under a consumption economy so far dedicated to the welfare of its membership as to make scarcity a virtual and unemployment a total non-starter. Some

* *What's Wrong With The Modern World?* (The Bodley Head).

conscientious trouble-makers would continue to gnaw away at what they are determined to smear as abuses, but how many less dedicated victims would bother to tangle with emergencies that have lost their momentum already.

Fear of Scarcity

The fact is 90% of all bloody-mindedness, lust for power included, is built on fear. And 90% of all fear – 100% in the case of economic theory – on fear of scarcity. Remove that fear by banning scarcity or the fear thereof and of the menaces tabulated above most would fold their tents like the Arab and silently steal away, leaving behind little more than a memory. A bad one. We steel ourselves to fight for rights and privileges that would automatically be ours had we planned our strategy with ordinary horse-sense, then stuck to it. As it is, every issue is so alienated from every other issue that even the massive intellects who do battle with such, while not admitting defeat, are fain to ask for more time; or an amnesty; or even an adjournment sine die. Thus Michael Shanks, who having listed these threats, dedicates the book to his ten children and step-children who will inherit them, he being with many apologies unable to come up with any remedy beyond a general hope for an improvement in human nature itself now that the example of an established religion, the great stabilizer, no longer functions. That point he has every right to make. Between them Christian poverty and Christian charity would make mincemeat of the lot; though in the present climate of opinion Providence if she is listening would be a very silly woman to set them up. He is surely right, too, in his diagnosis of wage inflation, though the punch-line could have been a reminder that it's the price we pay for the trade unions' heroic achievement in dragging the workers up into the middle classes; an act which is going to pay huge dividends in the not-so-distant future.

Trade unions are in fact laissez-faire institutions and have played an outstanding role in raising a genuinely degraded proletariat, once identified as the deserving poor, to bourgeois insouciance. A tremendous achievement which can only be impaired by the destruction of the bourgeoisie itself under the kind of planning whose troth is plighted to a socialized economy. Any political monolith is under necessity to reduce the unions to cyphers, will indeed do as the Russians have done; creating in the process a new road to serfdom for a new race of underdogs.

Unrestricted – meaning universal – laissez-faire is pernicious for exactly the same reason – it threatens the balance of the scrum; and for that reason alone the strict Adamic canon stinks to high heaven. But what its enemies fail to realize is that the laissez-faire is pernicious only because it is unitary and insofar as collectivism is also unitary, which of course it is, to that extent it also is pernicious and for exactly the same reason and to the same degree. Pernicious because, as the communists will one day discover to their serious discontent, by dislocating the economic triple alliance it reproduces the errors of the laissez-faire in hand-cuffing together two of its three trusty arms. Behind the back too, thus destroying the balance that keeps this mobile stabile.

The rule is the very simple one, here put forward more than once: offer the ox of private enterprise all the hay in the hay-net so long as he treadeth out the corn. But when the once willing beastie shows unwilling; when he starts to play not ox but ass – refusing, that is, to do the job he's paid to do – horsepower under an alternative management (C) must be called in to under-pin the silly cow. And let us add now that we are in the repeating groove, hopefully for the final time, that in the last resort capitalist or socialist makes no difference whatever so long as the one uses its opportunities to displace the other; neither being capable on its own individual initiative of providing a balanced economic *system* if only because a *system* requires by definition more than one component – in this case three. The error was endorsed, then officially ratified when the science identified itself – or, rather, Marx identified the science – with production and its relations, so narrowing the field to one only of three antithetic powers.

Ways, that is, of reacting to material conditions. Not until we reverse this mistake by resurrecting and not only resurrecting, reintegrating production with consumption and distribution – and their powers – will things start to go economically right. Of these, consumption (and its powers) is still the ghost in the machine; and will remain a ghost until reinstatement and realignment and reprocessing begin to provide the conditions that will send one crisis scuttling after the next like boy scouts confronted by a shop steward.

20

THE CRAZY MIXED-UP ECONOMY

Nationalization

Since the ground has already been gone over to the point of exhaustion, more hardly needs to be said. Except to repeat, hopefully for the last time, that the question of *powers* – where, who, how many and in what relation – is still the crucial factor in this debate. So long as production, consumption and distribution remain the three powerhouses of economic practice the science must accept them as its basic sources of energy and the dialectical nature of their relationship as a framework for the power game recurrent between them. Dictated, let us repeat, by their own role as controls.

And very remarkable it is that in the 200 odd years since the *production economy* of historic tradition began increasingly to lose the initiative no voice has been totally successful in calling the Adamic or Karlist bluff – confidence tricks of genius played to the accompaniment of the grinding of twin axes, both razor sharp. In consequence the strategy for the remarkable – and remarkably new – events that followed has never been agreed or even crystallized. Strategy, none; tactics by the bucketful; with Keynsian forays into enemy country never seen by the great tactician himself as more than a holding operation mounted to keep the foe at bay by brilliant guerrilla action until help came. Useful but provisional. An institution which reveals itself with some elan and alacrity as fundamentally triadic is asking for something more than delaying action or even a tactical offensive on conformist lines.

The retort will be made that *that* precisely, a strategy, is what our tribunes, conscious of some missing link in the economic scene, have set out to correct by the introduction of the mixed economy. For once the tribunes are right. A mixed economy we need and a mixed economy we have. A *mixed* economy. Yet not even the hardiest statesman can expect a mixed economy, sound though the conception is, to work a miracle until and unless someone, somewhere, sometime furnishes a blueprint for the mix. The which, believe it or not, no one has yet troubled to provide.

Upshot (to repeat an earlier conclusion), not a mixed but a mixed-up economy, like that crazy mixed-up kid's, beginning right at the start with nationalization. What madness can have possessed those fanatics to take enterprises out of the hands of entrepreneurs who know how to run them profitably in order to chalk up a huge national debt which you and I have to redeem in the name of an inefficient public service. As though nationalization were an end in itself instead of an unhappy necessity only to be embarked on when no one else will do the job.

To take goods and services out of the hands of men who have a talent for and interest in organizing these dreary matters on the lunatic argument that affairs will go better under simpletons without either talent or interest, who nonetheless believe nationalization to be 'right'; to go further still and switch all the rest of the jobs from one system to the other on the grounds that the answer to the partial failure of the principle must be total commitment to it, is really unbelievably mad.

Total socialism can only repeat the mistakes of capitalism and communism by reducing a triad to a monad and so ball up the whole system. The socialist cause needs the support of its opposite numbers, and far from taking work off rival shoulders should lose no opportunity to press every possible responsibility upon them. What in the shape of a C-economy the socialist cause can do is to evoke an alternative life-style to that of the P- and D-types by entering a field of operations no one else wants to be responsible for except in the way of charity. It would, in fact, undertake many activities of a charitable type – meals-on-wheels variety – with perquisites of various kinds for those providing the services – from jalopies to bed and board. There is a huge backlog of services the market sector just doesn't want to know about because costs would price them out of existence. And has. Who today can get the simplest article repaired? Pass this territory over to the C-arm – or State – or Crown, and presto – a fresh source of labour (in social terms free labour, in State terms cheap labour) is made available; with all that would mean in terms of maintenance, repairs, odd jobs, community work in general – not to mention its spectacular effects on inflation, rates and general taxation.

The Vocabulary of Contradiction

Which brings us to other words as understood today. One consequence of a crazy mixed-up economy is the crazy mixed-up character of the official vocabulary that accompanies and seeks to make sense of it, another symptom of a crazy mixed-up state of mind. Not only in the field of economics either. This book began with the puritan revolution and the efforts of the English Parliament under Millennial Yearnings to father on the West a new way of life rooted in a hitherto unattainable ideal. Current ideology dismisses their efforts as 'do-goodism' – 'good' having become a dirty word and the messianic dream of a good society, a meaningless one. A natural reaction in our present circumstances.

But definitely mixed up. A state of confusion not confined to the economic front though closely related to it, and responsible for extraordinary somersaults in the way otherwise mature people look at events. The puritan revolution for instance, the most significant event in English history, widely regarded today as an interruption in the stately progress of constitutional democracy and so a blackleg operation. Thus Dr. Cohn in the *Pursuit of the Millennium* already referred to, a work in every way typical of his age and ours. Does he admire that itch? He does not. For the Doctor that itch is murder. The source of all evil. Or nearly all. In his verdict he carries the modern approach – so odd and inverted as it will one day seem – to its natural conclusion – or confusion – by explaining with dispassion as frightening as it is lucid that because otherwise normal (meaning in his vocabulary ineffectual) people – Little Men – were filled suddenly with 'an intense and indefatigable energy' when offered a 'programme of purposeful action' aimed at overcoming the 'ineluctable limitations and imperfections of human existence', the symptoms *must* be morbid.

In the Doctor's view, observe, human limitations and imperfections are ineluctable. Ergo, anyone who rouses himself or urges others to overcome them is either fool, knave, or subject to delusions. As the disease rises to its climax this dope will develop a 'megalomaniac view of himself as the "elect"', attribute 'gigantic and demonic powers to his adversary', fall under an 'obsession with inerrable prophecies', all symptoms, which constitute 'the unmistakable Syndrome of Paranoia'. Funny peculiar in short . . . Anyone so perverted as to have the messianic itch and draw energy from it *must* be funny peculiar.

His next step is to relate all passional movements, religious or political or a combination of both, to the irrational fervours of our own day, in the baleful forms of Fascism, Nazism and Communism; beneath whose pseudo-scientific terminology one can recognize in each case, says Cohn, 'a fantasy of which almost every element is to be found in fantasies which were already current in mediaeval Europe'. In each case there is the 'final battle of the Elect' (be they Aryans or Proletarians) against the hosts of evil (be they Jews or Bourgeoisie). To primitive minds, believing in a world purified of evil, these ancient imaginings, now as in the Middle Ages, 'can function as dynamic social myths'.

Thus all the troublemakers throughout the history of Christendom, from the Nazis and Marxists backwards through the Ranters, Puritans and Cromwellian regicides to the Brethren of the Free Life and John of Leydon and the flagellants and Catherine de Hainault and the hosts of the People's Crusades, can be classed as victims of paranoia, and shown to share their fantasies with all the other victims of psychic conflict.

Ugly Enthusiasm

Stick to this, the entropic view of history, and with Doctor Cohn and other men of rectitude you will decide that under a wasting universe the political evolution of Flintstone man must be a thing of infinite slowness. And smallness. Supposing it to be there at all, progress if any will be almost invisible; taking, should it happen to happen, the form of a series of Little Steps by Little Men up Little Ladders, none of whom can be expected – the men, the steps or the ladders – to do more than mildly and passively and very littly breathe a few trifling ameliorations into the ineluctable imperfections of human existence. Evolutionary tempo bumped up it could be, but O what a little bumped up by the O so little Man. Such an outlook leaves no place in Little Men for Horace Walpole's 'ugly enthusiasm' which, when it occurs in such force as to be impossible to ignore, must be attributed (as he and Dr. Cohn and James I did) to an abnormal state of mind. Hence political convulsions are the record of the sudden development of paranoid manifestations, messianic fantasies and militant apocalyptic, probably dangerous, reverting sooner or later to 'revolutionary chiliasm, an approach to history both teleological and cataclysmic'.

Let us unwillingly admit that the Doctor and others who hold his views can produce evidence of some weight in support of their faith or lack thereof. Still, that isn't where the issue lies.

No one is likely to deny that the human race, generally under fear of scarcity, has often behaved with discredit to itself and its gods. The question remains whether it is committed by some inelectuble law of its own nature – or its deities' – to perpetual arrested development. In this dilemma every individual has sooner or later to take sides if only for the sake of his bank balance. And with burning enthusiasts pointing trembling fingers at better worlds, common sense (i.e. fear) causes perhaps 99% of the population – in the West, anyway – to dismiss all visionaries as victims of paranoia and other psychic conflict. This reaction is virtually inevitable, Darwin having a century ago handed us natural selection on a plate and so hammered the last nail into the coffin of free-will. After that no real alternative to passive acceptance of the human lot any longer existed except cynical contempt for it.

Not that these attitudes are mutually exclusive. Both represent facets of passive acceptance. And there the matter could rest but for the nuisance value of an insignificant minority who remain obstinately proof against either passive acceptance, cynical contempt, Cohnic delusion or Darwinian inversion. For these cross-grained characters evolution, far from being as most of its disciples imagine an organic principle, is purely and simply an intellectual device – for channelling the chaos of mental fantasies we call the past into a rational pattern satisfactory to the system-making gnome who inhabits the brain. Like formal logic, an intellectual frame invented for reference back, it has no application whatever to now or tomorrow in the sense that it can tell you what is or is not ineluctable vis-à-vis nature – or human nature. Triumph of human reason though it is, evolutionary theory has, to put it that way, nothing remotely to do with evolution. We are exactly what we will be. We become what we believe.

Seen in that light the phenomena of ugly enthusiasm are capable of another interpretation than the one Church and State have put upon them. Admit for a single moment that Church and State have since Anno Domini made a hideous mess of history, and the great upsurges of frantic men claiming century by century a way to Utopia less gruesome than the standard Establishment purge, can be seen as something other than paranoia: the refusal of free souls to deny their obvious destiny. To such free souls the Cohnic picture of the messianic fantasy or the apocalyptic urge is a travesty of the noblest ambitions of the race, more honourably described as the rage of man to fulfil himself in a society whose true objectives are continually thwarted by real-political considerations of State conceived in fear of scarcity. These battlers, when the issue lies between Doctor Cohn and the ugly enthusiasts of the frustrated centuries, have no difficulty in believing that the millennium is attainable – must indeed be attained by one means or another if we are to avoid genocide. It is after all no more than the art of living constructively.

The Alternative Society

Our economic troubles are similar in kind, insoluble only because we happen to approach them in a state of confusion brought on by a terminology itself confused and confused because the vocabulary has been conceived in the economic equivalent of original sin. Seeing everything the wrong way round. Starting (and for the present discussion ending) with automation and full employment, the basic headache of our day, notions which are as we have seen a contradiction in terms. This, the paradox that makes a rethink on our economic philosophy inevitable – the basic quandary inherent in high-tech – how to exploit the full potential of the machine without putting the whole human race out of work. Or, as the moral rearmer might put it, how to exploit the full potential of society without putting both out of work, machine as well as man. Under an advanced technology scientific progress is about to achieve 'something which all former ages dreamed of but none had been able to realize' (Hannah Arendt), the liberation from work which will in a few decades 'empty the factories and liberate mankind from its oldest and most natural burden, the burden of labouring and the bondage to necessity'. A great ideal; but where mankind's oldest and most natural wage packet is to come from Arendt doesn't bother to say. Her anxiety is for a class that has been stripped of cultural opportunities at the moment of potential freedom; ours, more earthy, teeters round the Ricardo Effect and the proposition, self-evident enough to the Luddites, that 'machinery and labour are in constant competition'. That the labourer stripped of his labour is stripped also of his means of livelihood by a system divided against itself; one voice insisting on full employment, the other, by automation, cybernetics, microchips and all the gimmicks of the technostructure, demanding as near as dammit total mechanization. As near as dammit total unemployment.

Yet if you go to exquisite lengths to deny human beings the right to earn a living by the sweat of their brow you will have to provide them with some alternative means of livelihood or prepare for trouble. So at any rate reckons the legislator who finds himself battling to provide full employment for those he represents within a system under contract to throw them out of work. And into Welfare. The Age of Redundancy. Guaranteed until further notice by silicon and other capital substitutes for labour in the field of automated production. In particular computerization which enables machines to take over huge areas handled heretofore by unskilled or semi-skilled or even managerial workers; with repercussions on employment which must surely fill our legislators with profound dismay. Some hold that wholesale devastation of the labour force could be avoided by the deliberate pursuit of a growth economy – still shorter hours, still higher levels of production – but such a policy would involve astronomical investment of capital with no guarantee of success. What *would* be guaranteed by any effort to maximize economic growth under an exploding technology is multiplication of exhaust fumes, Los Angeles super-smog, greater and grander pollution of seas, lakes and rivers from poisons, pesticides and the discharge of industrial effluents; together with dangerous depletion of global resources. Above all, the exhaustion of what economists call 'free goods' – air, water, land – already deeply in the red. Colin Clark's *growthmanship* and Misham's *growthmania* underline the dramatic dropsification that would overtake world order were society to hitch its wagon to a single-minded hotting up of GNP.

But what conceivable alternative have we got? As we have seen except for the backtrackers like Misham ('no-growth') or E. F. Schumacher ('Small is Beautiful'), or, needless to say, the communist world (whose remedy is a cage disguised as a curtain) no one has come up with an answer that promises to make sense, and this is because the issues involved are insoluble so long as their victims remain prisoners to confusion in the shape of exhausted economic formulae. Or mere Luddites throwing spanners in works. Schumacher's intermediate technology has a meaning for the Third World but in the First would make the machine a second-class citizen and so bring back the 'hand' and his wage packet, a course the machine is under no obligation – indeed has no right – to accept; entailing as it would a degradation of the Arendtist ideal which accepts automation as the means of handing back to the 'hand' the freedom of the hand. The inexorable confrontation, this, an either-or, or Push-me-Pull-you, which insofar as one ideal runs counter to the other (and it does) is edging the social body to a razor-edge of frustration that borders on neurosis.

Once more, the name of the game: *Confusion*. Still another example of what lack of a clear (never mind Grand) strategy has brought upon a society in the toils of a system break it doesn't understand.

Yet after all the issue is simple enough. Automation is a word meaning 'let's make it without human hands'. Full employment is two words meaning 'we all want to put our human hands to work because our wage packets depend on us working as human hands'. One or the other must win and, our culture being automative, the hands must lose. God be praised, says Arendt, automation is liberating hands. But if earning a wage means using or being a hand how does one earn that wage without using or being it? And, come to that, is it the hand one wants to use or the wage?

Not funny peculiar that last question, funny ha ha. To look to draw a wage for not bothering to be a hand steers clearly against the laws of God and man neither of whom ever engaged to reimburse the hand they didn't want for being unwanted. Outside that royal road to ruin, Welfare, only one possible solution suggests itself: to dispense with current conformities, orthodoxies, accommodations, by establishing a new equation between wage and work.

The consumption economy. As simple as that. Our mamma, the Queen, arranges to feed, clothe and shelter us in return for a firm offer to do the chores. Far in fact from a new – a very old – equation, once routine in that microcosm of society, the working family. Not to the exclusion of existing market practices either; simply an additional or alternative means of employment; a supplement, no more, to the present pattern of private enterprise whose streets are paved with gold as well as bad intentions. Even when employment and unemployment have become meaningless terms this beautiful triple economy permits one if so inclined to become as well as a chore do-er in the public, a wage-slave in the private sector (and so invest in a Japanese auto that remains mobile rather than some hardware from British Leyland whose products, three quarters of them anyway, call for repair in their first year of life). Still, the new arrangement will help BL too, who once out of the hands of 'hands' will be free to pull out all the technological stops in the pursuit of profits to make us rich instead of overstaffing with redundant strikers to make us poor.

Third World

Rather than go over old ground yet again let us in one sentence turn to the rest of our planet, and the situation where the West, now once more making a fast buck, will be poised to switch some of its wealth and energy to the aid of the Third World. The moment one community – and one is enough – Britain for preference, widely advertised as having failed to find a purpose in the post-war world – provides a precedent for others to follow, it should not be difficult to create a C-economy chain-reaction within the Commonwealth; and, later, within the Common Market. With consequences the almost fabulous nature of which will furnish us with the spring-board we need to furnish a sales story – no less – for the depressed and deprived peoples; something in the absence of a revelation or New Look no one has come up with on this side of the iron curtain. Yet could a way be found to improvise a tie-up between the two halves of an ideologically divided world, the situation would change dramatically in favour of the new initiative and us, its initiators. All the more so in view of the predicament our adversary is stuck with, whose offensive confronts him with a threat to himself greater than that to his adversary.

Why, is easy enough to understand. While death or takeover put a natural period to one-man dictatorship, group or gang 'protection' – the classic gangster ploy – can (see the Mafia) survive indefinitely so long as disciplines are strict and methods of control ruthless. Lenin achieved one, Stalin the other, by means of an ideology that included both, and something else equally crucial, a cause: in *the party's* case a call to perpetuate – more, export – its philosophy to the rest of the world, if necessary by force of arms; and so throw down a challenge no one can ignore. With bombs to back it up. 'As the original home of the first workers' revolution', writes Brian Crozier, founder and director-general of the Institute for the Study of Conflict (and monitor of the Third World War), 'the Soviet Union itself decides or claims the right to decide just what constitutes Marxist-Leninist orthodoxy. In practice therefore it is not just the ideology that is exported but Soviet power. To doubt the legitimacy of Marxism-Leninism would be to imperil the party's hold on power . . . so the ideology must be exported not only because of the export of it is part of the ideology itself but so that the world can be made safe for Soviet communism.'

He adds by way of warning, 'communists never give way', but is less explicit why. Why, however, turns out to be the nub or crux since here the weakness of Communist dogma lies. Conceived in fantasy the dictatorship of the proletariat, a concept never more than merely notional – or cosmetic – was by Lenin instantly transmuted into the dictatorship of the Communist, i.e. Managerial Party. A very different animal, if only because the dogmas of Marxism-Leninism no longer rule *the party, the party* rules the dogmas. Slanting them when necessary in its own interests while posing in public as their handmaid, and liquidating with frightening efficiency any who resist its claims. Today Communism and the Soviet future are both of so much less consequence than the caucus or junta who plot their course that the facts would be better served were the quote above to read 'so that the world may be safe for *the Party*'. The party is totally obsessed with its own survival. It has to be. Not unreasonably in view of the part *the party* played in institutionalizing Communism. Faith has no dimension, hence under attack it is the Institution rather than the Faith the Faithful find it proper to defend when defence is called for.

Nevertheless, though as an absolute monarch *the party* can only survive by destroying any opposition that would destroy *it*, a defensive strategy isn't enough in a situation in which by the nature of the case even on its own manor – let alone the world at large – *the party* remains in the minority. Which means that no option exists but to take the offensive unless and until *the party's* claims can be established on a scale so world-wide that none dare challenge its authority. Lacking which it remains a minority movement doomed to fold whenever the KGB gangs up with (for example) the army or the bureaucracy or the Church or the victims of the establishment or the USS's dissatisfied Rs to call its bluff.

It is this, the party's own dilemma rather than Communism or Soviet armaments that constitutes the real threat to both itself and the free world, the necessity *the party* is under to establish supranational authority – or perish. In any case appeasement and liberalization are out; only brute force can stop the mouths of critic or dissident. Hence the police state. Hence the Archipelago. Hence the KGB, the all-powerful instrument of repression, equipped with its own courts, prisons, labour camps, psychiatric wards, and even a private army (the Border Guards) besides special units within the armed forces; all designed by argument, advice, kindliness, terror, bribery, blackmail, murder and elimination of defectors, to suppress opposition – any opposition – wherever it shows a leg.

The party's main concern, in short, is with its powers of overkill rather than the plugging of the Faith, its own or that of fellow travellers. A strength and a weakness. By giving hard-liners the right to pull out all the disciplinary stops and leave no holds barred, a strength; a weakness because in lieu of world recognition the system demands suppressions so ruthless that any society however cowed – or collectivized – will rebel eventually in ways destructive of the institution itself.

Here, to repeat, is the real threat. Communists never give way because *the party* not only will not but *cannot* give way. *The party must go on* either to dominate world society in the name of Communism or to receive the chop in a struggle in which even allies are enemies so long as they refuse to follow the Kremlin's initiative.

But isn't world recognition a tall order? Hardly. If we take the way things are going today, virtually all Europe is either in or vulnerable to the Warsaw Pact including the members of the Common Market, some of whom like the Italians are already on the wobble. Brian Crozier makes a distinction between satellites and fellow travellers, but if you lump them together Africa is slipping fast into Soviet hands while America's defeat in Korea and Vietnam has made Asia more than vulnerable. With China already practising the same faith and South America flirting perennially with Communism, beyond the North and South Poles and of course Saudi Arabia there isn't much left of the world to win leaving aside the Anglo-Saxon communities all of whom continue to back-pedal industriously.

Seen thus Moscow's position looks rose-tinted. Yet the tint isn't quite so rosy as it looks. Stalin left a knot someone had to untie and Khrushchev, by decentralizing the bureaucracy based heretofore on Moscow, or, more precisely Big Brother, had a bash. There were minor triumphs, a reduction of coercion in economic as well as political life, easier labour relations, a more rational outlook in the management of industry. Such as they were, however, the reforms were not enough and he, Khrushchev, in turn had to be decentralized in favour of those who'd come to realize that this thing, decentralization, was less vital on the administrative than on the economic front. Hence a new ukase that threw the emphasis on the autonomy and profitability of each industrial unit, some of the moves lusty enough to warn observers of a trend towards the re-establishment of a market sector.

Premature. Yet the possibilities inherent in such reforms do give food for thought; as do the suspicions of the same observers that *the party* itself is tending to splinter into the classic political divisions of left (Maoist), right (Titoist) and centre (de-Stalinist). Providing, had implementation occurred, a would-be liberalizing main-stream. Alas the movement if it was one degenerated swiftly into Isaac Deutscher's *immobilisme*, the dread – and also classic – palsy or paralysis all tyrannies in time and place are heir to – how to relax the stranglehold, the archipelago, the police, the KGB, the prisons, the prison camps, the psychiatric wards, without inviting by such acts of conciliation a backlash amongst the victims and their extramural allies that would sweep away the whole edifice and the ideology that created it in a spontaneous act of vengeance. Remembering that under the lake's glasslike surface trouble of many sorts brews, with amongst other traumas widespread juvenile delinquency (unreported), a symptom of the boredom and frustration the system breeds. Denied guns or knives one gang long before all brollys were poisoned sharpened to points the ends of its own in order to do murder.*

Here is the headache *the party* can find no way to resolve except by stricter disciplines or world hegemony. Yet it is exactly this emergency which provides the West with the opportunity it needs. For action. Action of a novel kind. The traditional brand of aggro backed up by guns and threats is today as oldie-worldie as detente or containment or even Chichurin's peaceful co-existence, all of which become otiose in a situation where the adversary is the victim of his own *offence*. Nor, seeing that they are invariably misunderstood, does any future lie in simple acts of friendship.

However, since we know or ought to know by now where the practical trouble lies – in a maladjustment that, despite all dialectical materialist dogma and tradition, ignores the triadic nature of the economic instrument – here, it suddenly and surprisingly transpires, the initiative swings equally suddenly and surprisingly to the advantage of the open society provided it is geared to grab it; starting with the exposure of Karl Marxiavelli's unbeautiful strategem in fixing (in every meaning of the word) a straight fight between capitalism and socialism – between, that is, a D- and a C-economy – when both are integral components of a triple alliance. As soon as both parties realize that capitalist and socialist ploys oppose each other only in the sense of being complementaries and complementaries that not only *can* but *must* be carried on concurrently by way of mutual compensation, not only will the battle be over but the war won. With each participant claiming victory according to the light in

* 'There's only one sword, you know,' Tweedledum said to his brother, 'but you can have the umbrella – it's quite as sharp.' *Through the Looking Glass.*

which he sees his own contribution to the Peace Treaty. Founded, of course, on a consumer concordat which, handled diplomatically, could achieve electrifying results on the other side of the iron curtain, where it can be seen as a capitulation to socialism in the very heartland of the capitalist West; one *the party* could in turn represent to the Russian peoples as something even better, the last battle won. Victory for the cause. Victory for *the party's* cause. Offering thereafter under much back-slapping and swigging of toasts the opportunity for *the party* itself to make a determined lurch towards the market-place – even a private sector – in return for the unconditional surrender of the capitalist imperialists.

A welcome return; from poisoned umbrellas to old-world diplomatic humbug. For here lies *the party's* real means of escape. The mere establishment of market forces in one section of the Soviet economy will involve a huge relaxation of pressures in all the others. Involving in turn a whole new set of freedoms arising spontaneously from the nature of the exercise. Without (and this is the point) the threat of dangerous reactions amongst the liberated who will accept its intrinsically economic intention in naive good faith.

De-Stalinization on the economic front. The one foolproof way to relax existing disciplines without risk of explosion. A reciprocal move to that of the West – establishing an alternative economy at the other end of the spectrum.

Once the two halves into which the world has been ideologically split come together in a common economic philosophy that *offers the party* another opportunity to work its way out of the impasse Marx arranged for it, by putting its economic house in triple order our worst political problems will be over. No reason thereafter why by taking private enterprise to one of its bosoms *the party* shouldn't relax its own dogmas further by a final arbitrary act requiring every citizen of the USSR to become a member of *the party*, then *calling for elections within the party*. Collapse of the police state. One way or another this will have to happen, so we might as well try to accelerate the business by sympathetic action aimed at bringing East and West together in a common understanding of the principles of house management. Fringe benefit, an end once for all to the armaments race: four hundred thousand million dollars spent annually by the World on weapons of war. To be channelled henceforth one must hope into exercises that will aid the developing nations to build under the apron of the overdeveloped their own alternative societies and so initiate a spontaneous source of new world wealth.

This is where the British Commonwealth could somewhat to its own embarrassment play a new and crucial role in international affairs. There are still 900 million human beings trapped in what the World Bank in its first Development Report called 'absolute poverty'. So bedevilled, that is, by malnutrition, illiteracy, disease, high infant mortality, low life expectancy and the indescribable squalor of pavement or shantytown culture 'as to live beneath any reasonable definition of human decency'. Five Africans in six have no access to safe water supplies. One American baby consumes 50 times more of the world's resources than an Indian baby. Yet, says the World Bank, not poverty but greed is the spectre that stalks the earth, the greed of the West, generating loss as well as shame by an indifference that will quickly become damagingly self-destructive unless offset by aid and trade. A view supported by the UN which maintains that a percentage of every country's gross national product should be invested in the Third World. Britain's in particular, one might add, since three quarters of the 'absolutely poor' are to be found inside the Commonwealth, receiving from us about half the UN approved GNP figure of 0.70 (0.37 by the last count) rather less than Canada's, Australia's, or Scandinavia's but rather more than Japan's, Germany's or the USA's.

Aid and trade. These, some may hold, can hardly touch the surface of a problem rooted perhaps in greed yet not on that account susceptible to mere idealism or goodwill, let alone double-entry. Or even putting our money where our morality is will not, they maintain, save the whole problem. Fair enough. But does it follow that a productive economic philosophy can do nothing to help the good work on? Far from being unprofitable the right moves now could surely correct some of the false emphases directly favouring a very rich and a very poor world.

It was these corrections the communists sought to achieve with intentions we can all honour. Could indeed do more than honour – imitate – had their substitution of total socialism for total capitalism not, alas, repeated the very mistake made by the open society in opting for one and only one economic way of life. The economic way of life is not monolithic; is never monolithic; and now that the opportunity exists to put the whole business right it seems a pity not to grab it. An act of ordinary commonsense, surely, to exploit the system according to its functional pattern, thus providing *for the first time* the one sure and certain – the one quick and easy – route to higher GNP. Our own. But more auspiciously that of the emerging nations. At the same time offering the communist world something of even greater moment, a means of escape with honour untarnished from a philosophy whose only error is its logic, which relentlessly pursued must end in a shoot-out.

The first, indeed the only requirement, is an understanding of the tripartite nature of the economic system and the recognition that that system is being in some way abused. For proof we have the basic quandary we have explored already, under which mass production plus automation renders the workforce potentially redundant. No crime has been committed, no blame can be pinned on any breast; we are the victims of our own genius. And nothing but genius could have landed us in this excruciating quandary: a situation in which full automation and full employment, each in its own right an immaculate ideal, admit with sobs to being mutually exclusive.

Nor does the solution demand any sort of economic expertise; the conclusions offered here dispense with every aspect of the science except its first propositions. These in revealing a triadic structure (P, C and D) impose on its programmers a trinity of economic procedures; and so long as Malthus' 'first and greatest generalization' stands, one assumption *must* involve the others. No need either of lengthy demonstrations; that first premise establishes a dynamic dialectical process insensitive to formal logic.

21

UNECONOMIC MAN

An argument has to choose a theme and one theme is commonly enough for one argument though others may try and even deserve to crowd it out. In another epoch to claim priority for economics might have been to commit literary suicide but since Marx turned the standard approach to constitutional history arse-over-tip, form on the rat race-track has followed his lead.

Insofar as its author is capable of economic thought this book represents a slavish following of the fashion, without however taking the persistence of the fashion for granted; so by way of self-defence ends as it began with what some would hold to be the real issue, Dr. Collier's in the Putney Sermon already quoted and put to the Cromwellian top brass as the de-spiritualization of that fairyland above the clouds, the Kingdom of Heaven. Realize the thing on earth, he cried, bring it down from the clouds. Don't wait for the afterlife. *Not* Elysium, *not* Paradise, *not* Zion nor the Celestial City, admission to which can never be arranged until one's own departure from earth is sure. And even then, lest the deity takes umbrage, only by keeping the low profile described by the author of Psalm 131 where, as the translators put it, David professeth his humility (Lord, my heart is not haughty nor mine eyes lofty: neither do I exercise myself in great matters or in things too high for me). None of these. Quite an earthly paradise: the NU JU.

However, Dr. Collier's advice had snags, starting with the Common Human Pattern or CHP – until our own century so low in profile itself as to be in no shape to do battle for basic human rights, let alone give Heaven a whirl. Villain of the piece as usual none other than our old adversary, scarcity. The Church tried to solve the problem with its own economic equation – Christian *poverty* plus Christian *charity* = Christian *liberty*, i.e. even in the absence of a surplus, perfect freedom – but couldn't make the equation stick in view of earth's most intelligent animal Sapiens

Sapiens' conviction founded on hard personal experience that the life force doesn't work that way. Poverty it may acclaim; from charity it recoils as from an open drain, preferring rather to make the well-being of one party dependent on its ability to consume another. The spider-fly syndrome, embraced with hysterical joy – ecstasy even – by mature minds as ecological balance. Here Sapiens found to his dismay that he could only survive for three score years and ten by forcing the soil to succumb to grass which in turn was made to succumb to cattle whom he in turn could consume; gaining in the process the avoirdupois to corner a girl and cause her to succumb to a family of males vigorous enough to clobber the consumer next door and nobble his herd of kine for their own uncharitable ends – well aware though they were, and are, that this respite will do no more than postpone their ultimate surrender to the worm.

Consumption. Of one identity in the interest of another, whether a 'higher' or 'lower' form of life seems to be a matter to which Nature remains alarmingly indifferent. Unless one happens to think she regards the Second Law as crucial, in which case her main role can be seen as unraveller of that which she once knit up with care.

In face of this dread machinery Sapiens, who is au fond a do-gooder, sees little point in aiming at a ceiling higher than that of cattle rustler; though when enough of these bovine brutes feather – or leather – his bed he's been known to widen his horizon to include imprudencies called by C-types civilization and by P-types culture; neither of which do more than postpone his inevitable end; indeed often hurry it on.

Nevertheless the contradiction between his situation sub specie aeternitatis and his dependence on beef-and-two-veg is bound to raise crucial questions in the mind, and these might even be susceptible of an answer had the race an opportunity to figure one out. Alas, confronted with the prior need to survive few have time to close soberly with the problem, hence this extraordinary predicament – scarcity – still dogs us after sixty to six hundred millennia. Surely today with all this know-how, all this high-tech and industrial muscle we ought to be able to give scarcity a nudge and so free the field for more advanced studies. The issue is so simple. If the race can once for all create the machinery that will *produce* and *distribute* the necessary means of *consumption*, it will have time and opportunity to occupy its thoughts with the greater exigency.

Such, mainly, is the argument for putting our house – or rather van – the economy is after all auto-mobile – in order. This book does no more than suggest that the working principles should be understood by all. Not the difficult feat some might imagine, as we trust we have demonstrated.

Once the mechanics are mastered, once the wheels within wheels begin to whirr, we shall find that most of our problems outside the basic one (of 'life') are chimaeras that will depart shrieking; leaving behind a silence in which those who are still undismayed can compose themselves to enjoy the gallows music of *existenz*.

That business, however, some may find an ordeal more painful than the one it displaces. If so let them be comforted by the thought that it is for future shock. Current battlers will first have to face the problems involved in getting a consumer economy off the ground, which means nothing less than creating a culture complementary, in the sense of diametrically opposed, in the sense of antithetic (but not antipathetic) to that of the stockbroker belt. And isn't that precisely what a sizeable slice of our society is looking for: an alternative to the rat-race, with attractions of a more permanent kind? Some drop out, others turn on, still others look to supersede the existing disarray by an *alternative society*. Yet by whatever title one and only one realistic way exists to achieve it – a redeployment of the economic system that takes account of and seeks to activate its – the system's – own infra-structure. Stuck with a science of three antithetic impulses one must look for each to fructify as opportunity or (as Cromwell would say) providence knocks.

Opportunity today does rather more than knock. Sounds the alarm in the shape of solid-state technology right there by the bedside of the civil society where destiny's three-waveband digital alarm-clock-radio emits a rapid succession of electronic bleeps to the four syllables of *un*-em-*ploy*-ment what time our legislators, yearning to procrastinate, grab the snooze-button which gives them three minutes of extra time in which to remain asleep to the facts of life.

And three minutes is about as much snooze-time as Western society can now afford. Cromwell had a whole nation treading water for twelve years while he listened for providence's rapid succession of electronic bleeps – precisely the way he received that lady's messages surely – yet no such instructions turned up in an age where neither the time nor the solid-state technology was ripe. For us, conversely, even with the snooze-button hard down providence's alarums have become deafening in the face of an idea whose time has come; than which nothing in the world is more powerful. Be not deceived, reader, failure to respond to the bleeps of this opportunity can and will incur sorrows deeper far than the tears of woe foreseen in the prophetic jingles of William Blake.

Let us once more and for the last time restate the terms of this revolution. No revelation. No conversion. No change of heart or head, no new machinery of government or build-up of organization, no creation of a vast bureaucracy is required or intended. The bureaucracy is there. The machinery is there, the governing hierarchies are there, from the local council to the House of Commons and indeed the monarch. Only require-ment, that the citizen, his wife and child should decide to devote a few hours a day to the Queen on top of what they are already doing or not doing in their own interest and that of the private sector. In return for those hours spent serving Queen and country, their country will try to satisfy some of their basic needs. So played, the game of consumption economics or estate management will fulfil the players, enrich them, rob them of frust, and leave them free – freer anyway – to consider what are the real objectives of the good life. In which exercise they will at long last make contact with others, some of them long dead, who have had the same ambition; and so reintroduce a calculation that under the weight of universal *anomie* has almost ceased to exist.

And don't be taken in by North Sea oil or the world's biggest coal field; bonuses granted, but calculated to work to our long-term disadvantage so long as they water the roots of the two great weeds of our time, monopoly capitalism and nationalization which, far from rejecting, tend to twine each round the other with a double stranglehold in pursuit of the ultimate seizure. The oil and the coal by bumping up the speed will merely speed up the bump. For any bump-free future one must look to spend the lovely lolly that comes into the kitty by way of bonus on a radical and com-prehensive economic transformation; one that will turn the dole and welfare into a source of wealth by making both productive. The principle is of course as old as its Familiar Spirit, the family, but it has a new look for those who live in the shadow of redundancy. The Americans, masters as ever of the pragmatic approach, have already scented the need without bothering about the principle, as the *Daily Mail* for December 2, 1976, recorded in George Gordon's 'America' column:

> If you have trouble paying the rates and car road tax, consider the unique deal being offered in Hartford, Connecticut.
>
> The council there offers hard-pressed citizens an opportunity to work off the debt. Clinton Webb, a home-owner who has

been unemployed for 18 months, spent 40 hours a week repairing the city's fire engines.

Many other residents have temporary jobs as secretaries, accountants, mechanics and recreation attendants. None of the jobs could justify full-time employment and the council, rather than take on staff, puts out the vacancies to 100 low-income residents hard-hit by inflation.

Michael Donohue, a councillor and sponsor of the project, explained: 'Let's take a person who has been living in the city for 25 years. He owns a house and has been a loyal resident. Suddenly he's out of work and his property tax has got to be paid. We feel the city has responsibilities towards him.'

The city examined the people who were struggling and then matched 100 of them to the part-skills required. Mr. Webb, who worked off his tax debt over six weeks, said: 'I only have good to say about the programme. I wish others could get the same chance as I did.'

The indications are that they might. Several cities around the country including Boston, Washington, Mobile, Nashville and Atlanta are keeping a close eye on the scheme's progress. Worcester, Massachusetts – an hour's drive away – is on the verge of launching a similar work-your-tax-off.

Nicholas Carbonne, the councillor who started the scheme, admits: 'It is not the total answer, but it is a step in the right direction. It not only fills a need, but it alleviates some of the more serious problems that arise from being unemployed.'

The scheme has in fact achieved a lot more than the lowering of a city debt. It has given the unemployed a sense of pride and achievement and has a social impact on the community.'

The end product may not be quite as simple as this but details are for the specialist, including such matters as an alternative currency designed to make happy an alternative society. The thing that matters is to accept the principle as what it is, self-evident,* even though it may run counter to, for instance,

---

*A few months later (*Sunday Times*, July 31, 1977) President Carter from a peanut field claimed the existing welfare system to be anti-work, anti-family, unfair to the poor and wasteful of taxpayers' money. Before qualifying for any supplementary welfare relief everyone seeking cash assistance should, he proposed, be classified as *required* (for the fit) or *not required* (the aged, blind, disabled, heads of single parent families with children younger than seven) to take a job in the public service. This would have funds in the first phase to provide 1.4 million jobs for those unemployed however temporarily in the private sector.

Details may differ but the principle – and the ethic – agree that those who expect the State to help them should be ready to help the State. The Carter programme is scheduled for October 1988.

Adam Smith or Marx or the concept of welfare. Or current trade union practice; a resounding example of which was given in the *Mail* a week or two later under the headline 'NO GOOD DEEDS UNION TELLS SCOUTS'. It is reprinted here in the hope that this thumping union victory over small boys will rate some more enduring monument than printer's ink; a tablet perhaps at TUC headquarters.

Scouts who offered to clean up their local park have been stopped by the council workers' union.

The 50 youngsters hoped that their action would set an example to other young people and discourage vandalism.

But the secretary of the General and Municipal Workers' Union at Tonypandy in South Wales' Rhondda Valley is afraid that the Scouts would take the council workers' jobs away.

And now the local council have been forced to turn down the offer.

Mr. Ken Martin, leader of the 1st Clydach Vale Scout and Cub group, said yesterday: 'The lads have been doing community work for some time. They have been visiting old folk, digging gardens and fetching shopping. The old miners' recreation ground, which is now a park, is in a bit of a mess and the boys thought that if they cleared it up it might help to discourage vandalism. They hoped other youngsters would see their work and think twice before causing damage. They were not planning any regular form of maintenance – just to lick it into shape.'

Union branch secreatry Mr. Emrys Williams said: 'If we let Scouts do our work there is no telling where it will stop. Eventually all council work could be done by volunteers. We had to make a stand and tell the council that we would not accept offers from the Scouts or any volunteer group to do our work, which should be carried out by council workers. There is a shortage of council staff and we do not think the difference should be made up with voluntary labour.'

Rhondda Borough Council's Chief Executive Mr. Gwyn Evans said: 'Staffing levels in the parks department would not have been affected. We were forced to bow to union pressure. If not, we might have had trouble.'

A tour de force, you will agree, inviting amongst certain septs or orders actions which may oscillate between hurling the liquidizer through the kitchen window or being quietly sick in the sink. Promoting also the unpatriotic thought that the British may indeed have come to the end of the road. Time in that case if not already too late to call in the Americans, who when they realize what is at stake might be prevailed on to grab the initiative even when it seems on the surface to contradict their darlingest ideals. Others are of course involved besides the trade unions and our courtly but discarded scouts; in particular those youthful bad eggs and plug-uglies whose virtuosity in hooliganism, vandalism, violence, lies, theft and fraud is seen by fellow travellers as the haute couture of a psychotic age. Not without reason in the eyes of the social workers, who treat them less as truculent thugs than as the Stuarts and later the Hanoverians saw their own brand of mods and rockers (Independents, Congregationalists, Methodists, Levellers, Fifth Monarchists, Anabaptists, Agitators): disoriented.

Not to say deranged. In the words of Charles I 'passionate brains' and 'distempered persons' full of 'boldness and insolency of speech'. Charles, when he got the chance, didn't hesitate to crop their ears. Our own tyrants, the shrinks, look upon the current generation of young miscreants, probably rightly, as vicitims of a faulty balance within a Constitution whose slip is showing. Uncouthly enough as it turns out to call for redress – re-dress in the interest of the metaphor – re-dress by courtesy of a fresh foundation garment (or C-support), corrective not so much of the slip's slip as of the malfunction responsible for its original displacement.

However angrily and indignantly we may react to hooliganism or to trade union obstructionism, we can extract some hope from these disagreeable phenomena. It is an encouraging sign that the work-force of the country is now equipped to confront government, public, bosses, even the bureaucracy itself, with what amounts to an ultimatum on any matter within its brief, in particular the wage-packet. Which means nothing less than that the right to claim economic and in the last resort cultural parity with the middle classes has at last been won by the whilom sons of toil. Which means by the same token that following the mummification of the lords spiritual and temporal the middle class is rapidly becoming the only class there is. Whatever way you look at the class system, this means that class is on the way out, as it was destined to be as soon as the D-kids took over from the P-cocks.

An event of high significance for the future. Their strong-arm tactics may not be beautiful yet whatever disgust is felt for them, union misdeeds are largely an act of revenge, natural enough God knows, against those who once had the monopoly in ill behaviour and used it, the bosses.

Second, that whatever successes they pin up and however

impressive their victories, the unions belong by the nature of the case in the market place. Which means again that their tactics will by definition be fraught with the anarchist philosophy of the D-kids and the faith of same in a free-for-all.

Which means yet again that when as in their own self-interest they will be moved to do, the rank and file accept the mandate of the C-economy, both bosses and unions will find the alarms and excursions of the private sector inappropriate to the consumer ethic. Under nationalization withdrawal of labour from the Nation's life-lines in energy, communications, defences and the forces of law and order amounts, as the Russians were quick to discover, to mutiny, and must be dealt with as such (which is one of the reasons why we want a minimum of nationalization). On the other hand, under what to distinguish it from nationalization we may call national service – the right to all his numerous benefits under OAP, Welfare, Social Security – satisfaction of basic consumer demands will spring as it should do from his readiness to *give* a percentage of his time to the nation's service. He will of course, as in a democracy he must, have the right honourably to discharge himself from this service – from any service – to the Queen. But in that case the Queen may honourably discharge herself from her own responsibilities to him in the form of the benefits he would otherwise receive. The born outsider would prefer it this way.

Meanwhile until the overhaul of the economic wardrobe reveals the missing zip or link and replaces it with a new hook-up capable of re-dressing the balance, the slip will continue to slip.

Customer satisfaction however can be won easily enough by any genuine bid to tailor the gear to the requirements of the case. Example to follow here, none other than that of that august arbiter elegantiarum, Beau Nash, saint of haute couture, who prevailed upon the gentry taking the insalubrious waters of Bath to parade without their swords; so relegating the duel to the 'good old days'. If the same impulse were to move the crazy mixed-up nuts of these bad new ones to cast away their stink bombs and switch those four hundred thousand million dollars annually spent on armaments to the aid of the Third World how happy the First would be. Supplanting frust by trust and disunity by unity. As he of the low profile said (still on the theme of haute couture), 'how good and how pleasant it is for brethren to dwell together in unity. It is like the precious ointment upon the head that ran down upon the beard, even Aaron's beard, that went down to the skirts of his garment.'

Ointment. The ideal economic symbol, conceived as it was first *produced* for healing, then delight – or, as the economist would say, *consumption* – and by gravity *distributed* evenly over the whole fleecy system, yea verily right down to the skirts of Aaron's garments.

Without missing out on a single hair.

On a less fragrant note let us end with a word of advice to those hard-nosed types who, unmoved either by escalating armaments or Aaron's beard and its disposition to align itself with his garments, demand in their usual gravelly tones, what are you going to use for money? Answer. Once operative the system will be automatically self-supporting, indeed will make us all rich. Meantime, to get the show off the floor there is an annual £20 billion-plus of taxpayers' money screaming to be used fruitfully by those who for fifty years have been misappropriating the fund under the title of welfare and social security.